THE MYSTERY
OF LOVE AND
MARRIAGE

THE MYSTERY
OF LOVE AND
MARRIAGE

A Study in the
Theology of Sexual Relation

DERRICK SHERWIN BAILEY

HARPER & BROTHERS PUBLISHERS
NEW YORK

TO
MY WIFE

CONTENTS

PREFACE

A few years ago I contributed an essay on 'Clerical Marriage' to a study in clerical vocation entitled *Celibacy and Marriage*.[1] This book is an expansion of the pages in that essay which dealt in summary form with love and the idea of 'one flesh',[2] and little need be said about it by way of introduction. Although for nearly two decades its subject-matter has been widely discussed in theological circles, I venture to send it forth in the conviction that it treats of certain aspects of marriage and sexual relation to which little attention has yet been given. If it serves to direct the pastor and the theologian to them, and to initiate discussion, I shall be well satisfied. I believe that the grave sexual disorder of our time demands, in certain respects, a reorientation of the Church's attitude to sex and marriage, and in particular the development of a theology of sexual love; a clear distinction between what I have ventured to describe as the institutional and the ontological aspects of union in 'one flesh'; and a reinterpretation of love and marriage in terms of personal relation. I believe, too, that such a reorientation necessitates investigation into the sources and development of Christian ideas on sex and marriage, and a return of more favourable conditions in the publishing world may make this possible. The historical surveys in this study, however, had to be brief, and represent but a small part of the material accumulated. Hence conclusions have sometimes been stated (as in the case of the early Church) where the supporting evidence was too extensive to be given, while occasionally reference could only be made to one authority (for example, the *Summa Theologica*).

A word of explanation may be needed for the omission of

[1] 'Theology' Occasional Papers, New Series, No. 7 (S.P.C.K., 1944).
[2] To indicate its technical character, I have used this term in inverted commas throughout this study.

[ix]

any reference to contraception. I had intended to include an Appendix on the subject, but decided that nothing profitable could be added to the discussion at this stage. It is to be hoped that the report of the Commission on the Church and Planned Parenthood prepared for the 1948 Lambeth Conference, and summarized in *The Doctor's Profession*,[1] will be made available soon, as both its findings and the minority report are of great importance, and need discussion. For myself, I believe that the use within marriage of contraceptives in no way conflicts with the principles of union in 'one flesh' examined in this study, and may well assist the development of the personal relation between husband and wife—that is to say, I agree with the majority report of the Commission.[2] But at the same time I wish to make it clear that nothing in the pages which follow presupposes 'scientific' contraception: what is said, for instance, in Part II, § IV, concerning the frequency of intercourse holds good where only the 'safe period' is used.

While this study has been written primarily for Anglicans, as will be evident from the restricted character of the post-Reformation historical surveys, I hope and believe that it may prove interesting and helpful to others also.

It only remains for me to express my indebtedness to a great many friends for their help, and especially to Dr. David R. Mace for his encouragement and his unremitting efforts to secure publication of this study. The dedication is but a poor tribute to the continual assistance and advice of my wife, but for whom I should have understood little of the meaning of 'one flesh'.

D. S. B.

The Anglican Students' Chaplaincy
  Edinburgh
Easter Day 1950

[1] Ed. Daniel T. Jenkins, S.C.M. Press, 1949.
[2] See *The Doctor's Profession*, p. 55.

Part One

LOVE

LOVE

I

ALTHOUGH it is, in a phrase of Berdyaev, 'the ontological basis of the marriage union',[1] the love by which man and woman are united in that mysterious *henosis*[2] which the Bible terms 'one flesh' has received little attention or even acknowledgement from the theologian. Other aspects of marriage are treated at length, but upon this hardly a glance is bestowed. Not infrequently the theology of marriage has suffered in consequence, while the Christian conception of sexual relation has been sadly impoverished.

It is not difficult to understand the reason for this. The modern idea of sexual love was virtually unknown to antiquity. In pagan, Hebrew and Christian literature alike it is generally at best a kindly, good-natured benevolence or a personal affection grounded in *agape*, and at worst a powerful sensual urge or a fatal madness disturbing the equilibrium of mind and body. Exceptions of course are not wanting; there is evidence that men and women sometimes glimpsed and even attained a deeper level of relational experience than might have been expected under social conditions almost wholly androcentric. The Song of Songs bears witness to this, and so do the touching lament of Theius in the *Greek Anthology*[3] and the impressive *Laudatio Turiae*.[4] Cultural syncretism on the fringes of the Hellenic world led also to the emergence of a new valuation of woman and a quasi-romantic idea of love, which found expression in the New Comedy, the Novel and the work of the erotic poets. Much of this literature, however, was artificial, sentimental and escapist, and although it seems

[1] *The Destiny of Man*, pp. 302ff.
[2] *Henosis*—union, becoming one.
[3] *Selections from the Greek Anthology* (Mackail), Book iii, 51.
[4] See W. Warde Fowler, *Social Life at Rome in the Age of Cicero*.

[3]

to show the dawning of a new attitude, had no lasting effect. The old views persisted, and survived the break-up of the Roman Empire, finding new expression in the marriages of interest in which political expediency and not love was the determining factor.

Quite suddenly, however, towards the end of the eleventh century a change occurred, and for the first time account has to be taken of a new element in sexual relation—love, not as the erotic poets or the romantic novelists of antiquity conceived it, but more or less as it is conventionally understood to-day in Western civilization. The appearance in Languedoc of this Courtly Love (as it is usually described) was marked by an outburst of distinctive poetic activity, the songs of the troubadours, and it heralded a new attitude to woman which has had far-reaching consequences. The Provençal poets of eight hundred years ago

... effected a change which has left no corner of our ethics, our imagination, or our daily life untouched, and they erected impassable barriers between us and the classical past or the Oriental present. Compared with this revolution the Renaissance is a mere ripple on the surface of literature.[1]

Neither the origin nor the development of romantic love fall to be discussed here at any length. Dr. C. S. Lewis says:

The new thing itself I do not pretend to explain. Real changes in human sentiment are very rare—there are perhaps three or four on record—but I believe that they occur, and that this is one of them. I am not sure that they have 'causes', if by a cause we mean something which would wholly account for the new state of affairs, and so explain away what seemed its novelty.[2]

[1] C. S. Lewis, *The Allegory of Love*, p. 4.
[2] *op. cit.*, p. 11. Nygren, in *Agape and Eros*, II. ii. p. 442, makes the same point.

Whatever its source, the new idea in one form or another gradually permeated the whole of Western life and culture; romantic love has become an universal literary theme, and there is now no social level upon which it has not become established as an ideal, although in the course of popularization the ideal has not escaped debasement, and in personal relationship has usually been but imperfectly realized.

It is hardly conceivable that such a conception of sexual love as this revolution implied could have taken root in any ground but that prepared by Christianity, or could have flourished in any but a Christian atmosphere.[1] Yet for all this, theology remained almost impervious to romantic influences; the new movement of the Spirit did not, as it was once believed, owe or contribute anything to the Cistercian conception of mystical love,[2] though the sensual language and imagery of the *Minnelieder* and the Provençal poetry certainly affected the character of the *minne*-piety which was enthusiastically cultivated in the nunneries.[3] In one instance only can the effect of romanticism upon theology be seen; Peter Abelard treats of the love of God from the standpoint of one who had experienced the love sung by the poets, and declares that God 'is not to be loved as Abelard loved Heloise, but as Heloise loved Abelard'[4]—the pure love of God is love 'for his own perfection, even to the point of eventual renunciation of the beatitude he has promised us'.[5]

[1] See E. Gilson, *The Mystical Theology of St. Bernard*, p. 173.
[2] See the discussion in Gilson, *op. cit.*, Appendix IV, pp. 170ff.
[3] Nygren, *op. cit.*, II, ii, pp. 443-4.   [4] Gilson, *op. cit.*, p. 163.
[5] Gilson, *ibid.*, p. 161. The source of Abelard's idea is perhaps to be found in a passage from the first letter written to him by Heloise (Migne, *Patr. Lat.*, clxxviii, 184D-185A): 'God knows, I have ever sought in thee only thyself, desiring simply thee and not what was thine.... And if the name of wife seemed holier or more potent, the word mistress (*amica*) was always sweeter to me, or even—be not angry!—concubine or harlot; for the more I lowered myself before thee, the more I hoped to gain thy favour, and the less I should hurt the glory of thy renown' (see H. O. Taylor, *The Mediaeval Mind*, ii, pp. 12-13). Love, as Heloise conceives it, does not rest content merely with 'renunciation of its normal joys, but aspires to humiliation, contempt, provided that it would redound to the greater honour of the beloved'—Gilson, *op. cit.*, p. 164; here unmistakably the influence of the Courtly idea of humility is to be seen.

The Church was not entirely to blame for this failure to come to grips with the new concept of romantic love, and to work out its theological implications. The great period of Scholasticism had practically ended before the romantic idea had permeated European thought and culture to such an extent as to demand serious attention. So gradually, almost imperceptibly, too, had it woven itself into the pattern of mediaeval life that its challenge went unperceived. It dealt in categories for which theology had no equivalent, and was concerned with a situation in personal relation of which theology took no account, and of which the theologian himself was generally ignorant. When the Reformation set him free to learn by experience the meaning of the new love, he proved slow to take advantage of his freedom; hence the 'ontological basis of the marriage union' remained outside the scope of theology, and never received the attention it demanded.

While they do not discuss its nature and content, however, there were Anglican divines who have left on record a lively appreciation of the joys and blessings of married love. Thomas Becon, one of the first to judge that marriage would serve better to godliness, wrote:

The wiues loue is with no falsity corrupted, with no simulation abscured, with no chaūce of things minished. Finally with death only (nay not with death neither) withdrawn. She, the loue of her parents: she, the loue of her sisters: she, the loue of her brethren despiseth for the loue of you: her only respect is to you: of you she hangeth: with you she coueteth to die. Haue ye richesse. There is one that shal saue it: there is one that shal encrease it. Haue ye none: there is one that may seke it: if ye haue wealth, your felicity is doubled. If aduersity, there shalbe one, which may comfort you, which may sit by your side, which may serue you, which may couet your grefe to be hers. Do ye iudge any pleasure to be compared with this so great a coniunction:

[6]

If ye tary at home, there is at hand, which shal driue away the tediousness of solitarye being. If from home, ye haue one that shall kisse you, when ye depart: long for you, when ye be absent, receiue you ioyfully, when ye returne. A swete companion of youth, a kind solace of age. . . .

And this 'sweet fellowship' in which 'everything is common' is crowned with the gift of children:

Now sir, how highlye will ye esteme this thing, when your fair wife shal make you a father to a fair childe: when some litle yong babe shall play in your haull, which shall resemble you and your wife: which with a milde lisping, or amiable stammering shal call you Dad. . . .[1]

From the next century comes the testimony of Jeremy Taylor:

. . . when a man dwells in love, then the breasts of his wife are pleasant as the droppings upon the hill of Hermon, her eyes are fair as the light of heaven, she is a fountain sealed, and he can quench his thirst, and ease his cares, and lay his sorrows down upon her lap, and can retire home as to his sanctuary and refectory, and his gardens of sweetness and chaste refreshments . . . all the commandments of God enjoining a man to love his wife, are nothing but so many necessities and capacities of joy. 'She that is loved is safe, and he that loves is joyful'. Love is a union of all things excellent: it contains in it proportion and satisfaction and rest and confidence; and I wish that this were so much proceeded in, that the heathen themselves could not go beyond us in this virtue, and its proper and appendent happiness.[2]

It is unfortunate that men like Becon and Taylor did not go on to draw out the theological significance of the experience into which they had entered so deeply.

[1] *The Booke of Matrimony*, iii, Folio ed., fol. Dcl.
[2] *Sermons*, xviii (*The Marriage Ring*, Part 2), *Works*, iv, p. 224.

[7]

In addition to the cleavage between romanticism and theology another can be discerned between romanticism and secular tradition—the old utilitarian view of marriage, the old androcentric attitude to woman, and the old hedonistic, sensual conception of sexual love. For this, too, the conservatives were not entirely to blame. There was at first an element of artificiality in romantic love; it was the product of courtly leisure and cannot altogether evade the charge of escapism. In the beginning it was somewhat out of touch with the realities of actual sexual relationship, though this disappeared with popularization. But it proved difficult to resist the temptation to remain content with the contemplation of the new ideal of love and woman, to give it literary expression rather than to strive for its realization in the sexual relations of everyday life. This dangerous tendency has never been eradicated, and today, in a debased form, pseudo-romanticism of the most factitious kind exerts a powerful influence through the cinema, the novel, and the popular song.

Although from time to time there appear signs that the old androcentricity still survives, the cleavage between romanticism and secular tradition in sexual relation has virtually disappeared. Equality of franchise and the removal of most if not all the legal and social disabilities of women are only two of the results of the permeation of Western civilization by the romantic idea. Art, convention, and feeling alike bear witness to the magnitude of the revolution effected by the eleventh-century movement of the Spirit. But between romanticism and theology the cleavage has remained, though it is less pronounced in Reformed and Anglican thought than in Roman, where the Augustinian-Scholastic tradition continues with but little modification or enrichment. The climate of Christian thought in the West, however, has undergone a marked change, especially within Anglicanism. Christians individually accept the romantic idea of love, and the influence of romanticism is often to be seen in the presentation and even the

interpretation of the received teaching on marriage. But the Church has been unable to prevent the secularization and debasement of the romantic ideal. The consequences of the failure of theology to take due account of romantic love may be seen in the neopaganism of the Italian Renaissance. The eroticism of antiquity was misunderstood, and was interpreted in terms of an entirely alien romanticism to those who were seeking to relate the new but already developed conception of sexual relation to the concrete situations of the personal sexual life. That there seemed then to be no middle way between 'puritanism' and licence was due to the fact that romanticism had been allowed to become purely a secular force. The Reformation mitigated but did not remove this anomaly, and even in modern times we have seen the Church somewhat hesitant in asserting itself against secularism in such matters as sex education, and in resisting the insidious encroachments of pseudo-romanticism. This has been due partly to the fact that theology has been ill-equipped to meet secularism and materialism constructively on their own ground where sex is concerned, and in particular, to acknowledge and bring within a theological context the love which is the foundation of the marriage union. The cleavage still remains, and it is the purpose of this essay to suggest some ways in which the problem may be approached, and to put forward a reinterpretation of love and marriage.

II

IF confusion is to be avoided, the character and meaning of the love which is 'the ontological basis of the marriage union' must be clearly indicated. Very often its context alone determines the sense in which the word 'love' is used. Thus, it is possible to meet with two such contradictory statements as Berdyaev's, quoted above, and Brunner's: 'where marriage is

based on love all is lost from the very outset'.[1] Examination reveals that Berdyaev and Brunner are concerned with different conceptions of love—conceptions implied by the context, but not expressly stated—and that each, as he understands 'love', is right. This sort of contradiction, which is always occurring, is due to the use of 'love' in some sense which has never been precisely defined, but only subjectively determined. Nor is this the only kind of confusion to be encountered; the same word has perforce to do duty in English both for the love of Robert and Elizabeth Browning or of Peter Abelard and Heloise, and for the sentimental, trashy emotion of the film and the novelette—and for every shade of meaning between the two.

The difficulty cannot be met by any expedient so apparently simple as the framing of a comprehensive definition of this ontological love, for no definition could embody at once its complexity and its distinctive character. Only by analysing the total experience, so far as that is possible, and then considering in turn its constituent elements, can love be understood, and this is the method adopted in the pages which follow. An analysis of this kind cannot, of course, pretend to be complete, but at least the principal features of sexual love can be isolated and described. But the order in which they are examined here is not that of importance, and no single element can be said to confer upon the whole experience its evident *sui generis* character; nor do all the features mentioned relate exclusively to the sexual love which is the basis of the 'one flesh' union.

III

LOVE may first be considered in terms of personal relation, as a metaphysical experience which can best be described in Martin Buber's now familiar categories of *I* and *Thou*. Marriage, he says, springs from the

[1] *The Divine Imperative*, p. 344; cf. pp. 356ff.

. . . revealing by two people of the *Thou* to one another. Out of this a marriage is built up by the *Thou* that is neither of the *I*'s. This is the metaphysical and metapsychical factor of love, to which feelings of love are mere accompaniments.[1]

For Buber, the *Thou* is a subject which can be *met* (that is, with whom it is possible to enter into personal relation) but not *experienced*, whereas the *It* is an object which can be experienced, but with which it is impossible to enter into direct personal relation. The *I* likewise is a subject, and the 'world of *Thou*' is the sphere in which personal confrontation and relation occur between the *I* and the *Thou*. The 'world of *It*', on the other hand, is the sphere in which the *I* stands over against the *It* as subject to object, experiencing and appropriating, but never meeting in direct personal relation.

The meeting of two *I*'s is no irrational, impulsive coming together; in the encounter of lovers it has no connexion at all with the fatalism of passion.[2] However rarely it may appear to be deliberate, it is always in fact an act of choice:

The *Thou* confronts me. But I step into direct relation with it. Hence the relation means being chosen and choosing, suffering and action in one . . .[3]

This is of great significance if the love of man and woman is to be properly understood.[4]

What Buber calls the 'eternal' character of love is due, not to a pseudo-romantic escapism which would repudiate the 'vanity', the contingency of our temporal state, but to the entry of man and woman into the world of *Thou* which is 'not set in the context of either [space or time]'.[5] In the unique relational event of falling in love the woman[6] whom a man

---

[1] *I and Thou*, p. 46.   [2] See Appendix I.   [3] Buber, *op. cit.*, p. 76.
[4] Buber's terminology will be used without further comment; it is now familiar and is indispensable. For an exposition of his theory of relation the reader is referred to *I and Thou*.
[5] *op. cit.*, p. 33.
[6] All that is said here, from the man's point of view, of woman as *She* is, of course, equally true, from the woman's, of man as *He*.

loves (objectively *She*, someone to be experienced and evaluated) becomes *Thou*; and in this *I-Thou* meeting both enter into the eternity of the world of *Thou*. But this experience of love's eternity is only for a moment, when 'time stands still', though the moment may recur again and again.

> Love itself cannot persist in direct relation. It endures, but in interchange of actual and potential being.[1]

> The particular *Thou*, after the relational event has run its course, *is bound* to become an *It*.[2]

Herein lies one distinction between Divine and human love; for God, the *Thou* is eternally present; for man, the *Thou* tends always to lapse into *He* or *She*. Thus there is in love a continual alternation between the states of *I-Thou* and *I-It*, and the intensity of the experience, and especially of certain moments in it, bears a direct relation to the frequency of alternation. This is a necessity, not a defect of the relation. Because love has a proper concern with objective value, the beloved must become *She*: only so can she be compared, evaluated, and experienced, and therefore known as desirable—as more to be desired than all others. It is during her relapse from *Thou* to *She* that the lover becomes aware of the beloved's qualities, that he sees her as 'fairest among women'; in the recurrent *I-Thou* relation all objective particularity is swallowed up in the experience of meeting in personal encounter.

This explains the difference between the lover and the onlooker, a difference to which reference will be made again later. To the onlooker the beloved is always a *She* who may for one moment become for him a *Thou*; to the lover, she is a *Thou* who, though continually relapsing into objectivity, into the state of *She*, as continually becomes *Thou* again—for her relation with him is a relation grounded in the world of *Thou*.

[1] *op. cit.*, p. 17; cf. p. 99: 'Love itself cannot persist in the immediacy of relation. . . . Every *Thou* in the world is enjoined by its nature . . . to re-enter continually the condition of things.'
[2] *ibid.*, p. 33.

This alternation in relation is of great significance in the life of lovers and of husband and wife as 'one flesh'; it is inevitable, being a consequence of man's temporality, but upon its frequency the quality and duration of love largely depend. There can be no love without the experience of meeting in personal relation, and that is impossible where the other is merely an object, part of the world of *It*, and is allowed to remain so. And with the loss of true personal relation goes all participation in the *Thou* of eternity. Buber's quotation, ' "When a man is together with his wife the longing of the eternal hills blows round about them" '[1] is only true, therefore, if 'together' means united in a relation which is rooted in, and continually recurs to the basic *I-Thou* which belongs to eternity, and is not set in the context of space and time.

IV

THROUGH the relational event in which the beloved first becomes *Thou* instead of *She* there is mediated a 'vision of perfection'. This vision is no rare experience, but accompanies every genuine and complete falling in love, and may even follow, in a different way, from the relational meeting between man and man or woman and woman—though with the latter we are not concerned here. It has been described with great authority and insight by the poets, but has not escaped degeneration into the conventional artificialities of the dance 'lyric' and sentimental song. Even there, however, the attribution to the beloved of a sort of perfection (regardless of the standards by which it is determined) bears witness to a common and authentic experience. Often it is only through such amatory banalities that the great mass of the wholly or partly inarticulate can express at second hand what is for them, as for others,

[1] *op. cit.*, p. 103.

something intensely moving and significant. In a more sensitive and polished way the highest levels of poetry sometimes exhibit no less a reliance upon conventional imagery. Occasionally there is evidence of a struggle with both the idea and the medium;[1] occasionally the experience receives assured and masterly expression.[2] But nowhere has the vision been recorded and analysed more completely than in the writings of Dante, which have been interpreted with such authority by Charles Williams. It is inevitable therefore that any consideration of this experience should begin with Dante's meeting with Beatrice and her 'blessed' salutation, as they are described in the *Vita Nuova*. For a commentary in detail upon this significant encounter the reader must turn to Mr. Williams, to whose work my debt will be obvious.[3]

For Dante 'a kind of dreadful perfection has appeared in the streets of Florence; something like the glory of God is walking down the street towards him'.[4] Though others might have expressed it differently, his experience so far was normal and not uncommon. But Dante proceeded from experience to analysis and exposition; the full significance of the everyday event was set forth with unique precision and insight. Nothing calls for comment in this, except that it was possible without diminishing in any way the wonder or 'romance' of falling in love. The vision has its intellectual aspect, which must not be neglected if the significance of love is to be fully appreciated.

It is important to understand the sense in which 'perfection' is attributed to the beloved. It is essentially a perfection known only in the vision and for the purpose of the revelation mediated through the vision. Obviously the beloved is not, and cannot be perfect in the strict meaning of the term. The perfection which the lover sees, therefore,

---

[1] As in Shelley's *Epipsychidion* (1-123).
[2] For example, Milton, *Paradise Lost*, viii, 546-59.
[3] See especially: *He came down from Heaven*, ch. V; *Religion and Love in Dante*; and *The Figure of Beatrice*. I am glad to be able to acknowledge Mr. Williams' influence, and his kindness in permitting me to make full use of his works.
[4] *The Figure of Beatrice*, p. 20.

. . . involves no folly of denial of the girl's faults or sins. The vision of perfection arises independently of the imperfection; it shines through her body whatever she makes of her body. Thus chastity is exhibited in the lecherous, and industry in the lazy, and humility in the proud, and truth in the false.[1]

Apart from the vision the beloved is known objectively, as she is—that is, one *She* among others, perhaps better, perhaps worse than they. But in the vision she is seen no longer as part of that world in which evaluations and comparisons are made, because the vision itself belongs to the sphere where relative values are obliterated in the meeting of *I* and *Thou*.

Although, therefore, it is neither absolute nor strictly objective, the perfection disclosed in the vision is no romantic illusion. It is a potential perfection—a perfection to which the beloved has not attained, but to which, by the grace of God, she may be brought. The vision reveals the possibility of a new life, and is accompanied by a momentary but none the less real experience of a restoration of nature. It

. . . flashes for a moment into the lover the life he was meant to possess instead of his own by the exposition in [the beloved] of the life she was meant to possess instead of her own.[2]

God's mysterious purpose in Christ is made known in terms of the individual life, and His will for lover and beloved is declared, though it still remains to be done, in and by them both. There is no restoration apart from grace and faith and persistent endeavour, but if they have seen the vision and have understood, they know at least that restoration is possible. Thus, through the encounter of lovers, the mystery of God's will and the destiny of man in Christ are proclaimed. The

[1] *The Figure of Beatrice*, pp. 63–4; cf. p. 35.
[2] *He came down from Heaven*, pp. 96–7.

perfection seen in the vision is the perfection of man recreated after the pattern of the Second Adam.

The vision and the revelation are exclusive, and concern none but the lover and the beloved; that is why love is often quite incomprehensible to the onlooker. Sometimes it seems the most natural thing in the world that a man and a woman should fall in love, but not infrequently there is to be heard the comment: What can he see in her?—the onlooker being incapable of seeing anything to explain the relationship. The comment, of course, is meaningless: the onlooker cannot expect to *see* anything, for seeing is the vision, and that cannot be for him. To the onlooker, the beloved belongs to the world of *It*, and she is accordingly assessed by conventional standards at her 'face value'. But to the lover she is *Thou*: through the relational event of falling in love, with its vision of perfection, he has seen her, not as she is, but as she may become by the grace of God—and he cannot forget what he has seen. She has been revealed as God made her to be and wills her to become, and she is loved both as she is and as grace may remake her. Love is not blind, but exceptionally clear of sight; only the lover regards the beloved's faults and sins from a standpoint which the spectator does not and cannot share. In de Rougement's saying: 'To chose a woman for wife is to say to Miss So-and-so, "I want to live with you just as you are" ',[1] there is profound truth, once it is realized that because of the vision the lover's 'just as you are' takes account of potentialities which have been hidden from all but him. To the spectator, however, 'just as you are' can imply only a subjective judgement passed upon one who by predetermined standards, personal or conventional, has been evaluated as *She*.

In this vision the lover also sees reflected in the beloved something of the perfection of God, who according to their limited capacity reveals Himself and can be known in His creatures, and specially in man, His image and likeness.

[1] Denis de Rougement, *Passion and Society*, p. 314.

Because of the particularity of love, however, the beloved appears to the lover, not as one image of God among many, but uniquely for him as *the* image of God. Man has so been created that it is normally his nature to fall in love, and through that experience to see his Creator's perfection mirrored in the beloved through whom God reveals himself to the lover. When the falling in love is mutual, the lovers communicate to each other a vision of God who is the end of their love and their life.

> Every particular *Thou* is a glimpse through to the eternal *Thou*: by means of every particular *Thou* the primary word addresses the eternal *Thou*.[1]

> He who loves a woman, and brings her life to present realization in his, is able to look in the *Thou* of her eyes into a beam of the eternal *Thou*.[2]

Falling in love and the recurring encounters of love become moments in which the eternal *Thou* is revealed, since true relation between an *I* and a *Thou* means being brought, not only into a mutual relation, but into a common relation with the living, Divine Centre. The context of the world of *Thou* is not space or time, but

> . . . in the Centre, where the extended lines of relations meet—in the eternal *Thou*.[3]

Not only is the vision a revelation, through the beloved to the lover, of the perfection of God; it is also a means whereby both experience God, for their love is rooted in their relation with him.

The perfection made known in the vision is not only a potential moral perfection; it foreshadows also the integration of lover and beloved in their perfect union as 'one flesh' which

---

[1] Buber, *op. cit.*, p. 75.   [2] *ibid.*, p. 106.   [3] *ibid.*, p. 100.

is the end of their love. One purpose of the *henosis* is the establishment of a balanced and fruitful androgyniety in place of the disruptive androgyniety of the solitary and unintegrated man or woman. In the completing of each lover by the other the tension of strife between the androgynous elements in the personality of each is resolved and converted into a tension of repose. Both become fully integrated in themselves, and also integrated together in the 'one flesh' where the full meaning of love is realized.

The lover feels that through this vision of the beloved's perfection he has been given an ineffable perception of the meaning of things. The very sight of her

> . . . arouses a sense of intense significance, a sense that an explanation of the whole universe is being offered, and indeed in some sense understood, only it cannot yet be defined. Even when the intellect seems to apprehend, it cannot express its purpose: 'the tongue cannot follow that which the intellect sees'.[1]

In terms of relation the beloved, the *She*, has become *Thou*; she 'fills the heavens' and 'all else lives in [her] light'.[2]

Not only is the beloved the means of a significant illumination of the intellect, but she appears also as

> . . . the pattern of man's essence existing in thought within the divine mind . . . she is as completely perfect as the essence of man can possibly be'. She is, that is, the perfect centre and norm of humanity; others exist, it seems, because and in so far as they resemble her virtue. The extraordinary vision is that of the ordinary thing *in excelsis*.[3]

The beloved represents an ideal of creaturely perfection; she even seems to be 'unaffected by time'. This quality in her

---

[1] *He came down from Heaven*, pp. 92–3.   [2] Buber, *op. cit.*, p. 8.
[3] *He came down from Heaven*, p. 93.

springs from the 'metaphysical association of the visible light'
—the 'light that lightens every man that comes into the world'
is made 'visible through her, by the will of grace. . . .'[1]

Finally, the beloved is revealed in the vision as

> . . . the Mother of Love—of *caritas*, and even of a *caritas*
> beyond any *caritas* we can imagine; she is the chosen Mother
> of the goodwill of God.[2]

So she awakens charity in the lover; he feels a sense of well-
disposition towards everyone, so that even forgiveness is a
necessity. This experience of possession by *caritas* is in some
degree or other common to all lovers, and often finds expression in an increase of courtesy and refinement.[3] Sometimes,
admittedly, the experience may not last long, yet even so, it
may serve to awaken the realization that a new life and a new
basis of relation are possible.

The love which gives inward validity to the 'one flesh'
henosis demands a mutual, though not necessarily simultaneous,
vision of perfection, but it is important not to dogmatize
concerning the occurrence of the vision. There is 'love at first
sight' and there is mutual 'love at first sight', though such
experiences are not so common as amatory convention insists.
In most cases the vision happens, not at the first encounter,
but after a period of more or less intimate friendship, and the
man and the woman rarely experience it together. But where
the vision is wanting there is no true love and therefore no
inwardly valid 'one flesh' union. The vision cannot be organized, and may occur at any time—even after marriage—though
it would be wrong in the extreme to marry in anticipation of
it. To establish by sexual intercourse a state of 'one flesh' with
someone through whom the Divine glory had never shone is
comparable to prostitution; subsequently the vision may

---

[1] *He came down from Heaven*, pp. 93 and 94.
[2] *ibid.*, p. 97; cf. *Religion and Love in Dante*, p. 11; *The Figure of Beatrice*, pp. 21–2.
[3] Cf. C. S. Lewis, *op. cit.*, pp. 34ff.

ratify and procure pardon for the union, but to contract it on that assumption is indefensible. The vision alone can justify the act by which the *henosis* is set up.[1]

Although the vision is integral to sexual love and union in 'one flesh', it has no exclusive association with either. It proceeds, rather, from the supersexual relational event of personal encounter, and is a transcendental experience which may occur between man and man or woman and woman.[2] Nor is it a once-for-all experience. It may recur frequently; in rare cases there may be an almost continual sight of it. It is never an infallible sign that marriage is indicated, but there can be no inwardly valid *henosis* without it. The vision may even be mediated through another in circumstances which constitute a severe test of fidelity, for it depends upon the wholly incalculable meeting of the *I* and the *Thou*.

But the problem of the disappearance of the vision has to be faced. At the time it will seem to the lover impossible that it should be transient, yet so it proves to be. Although it is seen in and through a relational event (falling in love) it is not integral to the relational meeting of lover and beloved; it may recur, and recur often, or it may not. Its withdrawal, therefore, cannot affect the 'systolic-diastolic' alternation of relation in which *I-Thou* and *I-It* for ever succeed one another. To expect or to demand the continuation of the vision is unrealistic. It has its purpose and fulfils it, and it serves a purpose even in being withdrawn, whether for a time or for ever.

[1] Brunner's remark in this connexion is apposite: 'The love which is supposed to "come of itself where true Christians marry" belongs to the sphere of Christian legend'; see *The Divine Imperative*, p. 360.

[2] For a suggestive expansion of this point, see *The Figure of Beatrice*, pp. 15–16 and 63.

V

THIS brings us to the question of fidelity in love. Brunner says that the stability of marriage is based 'not on love but on fidelity. Fidelity is the ethical element which enhances natural love'.[1] This dichotomy between love and fidelity is, of course, due to the sense in which Brunner understands love, and upon this I have already commented. If love is ontologically both the basis of the 'one flesh' *henosis* and a permanent element therein, fidelity, the guarantee of its permanence, must be an integral feature of love; in fact, it is indispensable to the monism, the singlemindedness, which Brunner himself claims to be characteristic of 'genuine natural love'. Otherwise there can be no sincerity or even meaning in the words which love implies: 'it is with this particular person that I wish to live alone and for always'.[2] Once fidelity has been accepted as essential to love, even the withdrawal of the vision and the fading of the glory with which it had invested the beloved are seen to have their significance. They are a necessary stage in the progress of love, since they create the occasion and the need for the development and exercise of this essential fidelity.

But fidelity to the vision during the time of its withdrawal—and therefore to the beloved through whom it came and in whom the glory was seen, and to God, its ultimate source—is not required only of those who have consummated their love and have become 'one flesh'. It is demanded from all lovers from the very moment they accept their vocation and know that thenceforth their lives are bound together in a single destiny. Even in the case of a unilateral love-experience an obligation to remain faithful to the mediator or mediatrix of the vision *may* be regarded as absolute and life-long. The essence of fidelity may be said to consist in treating as unconditional *in its own sphere* the claim which (under God) lovers are entitled to make one upon the other, and in the ordering of

[1] *op. cit.*, p. 357.　　[2] *ibid.*, p. 347.

their lives with constant reference to the single centre around which (under God) their individual, personal lives revolve— the idea of love which they have built up, which enshrines all that is most precious in their relational experience, and to which they are bound in allegiance.

VI

To the relational event in which the vision is seen no sexual implication is necessarily attached. But the whole love-experience initiated in that meeting tends towards and looks for fulfilment in the physical sexual act by which the 'one flesh' *henosis* is established, and the physical sexual element is always important in the relation between lovers. They are always aware—sometimes acutely aware—of each other's sexuality, for an instinctive sexual attraction is the primary and most powerful feature of love. When allowed free course this attraction generally ensures the mating of those who are sexually compatible, although sexual compatibility, important as it is in conjunction with other factors, is quite insufficient by itself to ensure a true and fruitful love or a successful marriage. God's vocation of man and woman to union as 'one flesh' is partly indicated by the mystery of sexual correspond-ence; in love a principle of selection generally operates to secure the union of those who are physically compatible, and there is a real sense in which they can be said to have been 'made for one another'. But the false romanticism which asserts that for each there is one destined partner and one alone must be repudiated; it is one of the dangerous illusions which have contributed to the contemporary sexual disorder.

Almost from the first it is normal for lovers to seek expres-sion through the intimacies of physical contact. This is natural and inevitable, for they find that their deepest feelings and assurances demand a medium of communication more flexible

and delicate than speech. These instinctive intimacies are certainly sexual, and have their origin in the sexual attraction which is a basic element in love. But though they may often resemble to some extent the sequence of acts which generally precede and culminate in sexual intercourse, they are done in a different context, and within the limits proper to erotic expression between the unmarried are not to be deprecated or condemned. It is right and natural for lovers to take pleasure in their physical natures, and any constraint, coldness, or distaste for the normal and innocuous endearments of court-ship may indicate a degree of sexual incompatibility which would prove disastrous in marriage. But nothing said here must be misconstrued; only too easily can one thing lead to another, and limits must be set and strictly observed. There is a world of difference between pre-marital sexual licence and the reverent, restrained, yet natural physical intimacies of the lovers who understand the meaning of responsibility and detachment, who know the power of the sexual impulse, and for whom the physical is only one element in the love by which they are united.[1]

VII

THE vocational aspect of love has already been mentioned; various factors combine to emphasize that all true lovers receive each other at the hand of God. In the vision of per-fection, in sexual selection, and in relational experience, the Divine calling is made known, as well as in those many circumstances in which the Christian will see the purpose of God, and the non-Christian unaccountable coincidences or strokes of good fortune. But this Divine vocation is often misunderstood as the operation of some fate or destiny in obedience to which lovers are thrown together, and this

[1] In this connexion see the important remarks by Dr. J. R. Oliver in *Psychiatry and Mental Health*, pp. 203ff.

fatalism is encouraged by the irresistible, sometimes almost demonic power of sexual attraction and emotion. Men and women feel that control has passed out of their hands, and that they act under the compulsion of an inexorable destiny against which they are powerless to assert their own wills and exercise the responsibility demanded by true love. Insistence that love is Divine vocation and not fatal destiny can alone dispose of this dangerous and barren fatalism which has been extensively exploited in literature.

In this connexion it must not be forgotten that love is fundamentally the result of the extensive activity of the life-giving and unifying Spirit of God, who draws lovers together and unites them in a unique and mysterious relation. Consequently it is invested with a real natural sanctity.

Since love is a Divine vocation and the work of the Holy Spirit, it demands of lovers a great responsibility to and for one another; it is 'the responsibility of an *I* for a *Thou*',[1] and is received direct from God, to whom they are ultimately answerable for what they have made of their love.

VIII

IN the total love-experience three kinds of love are to be distinguished, typical of three different relations. They may be termed *eros*, *agape*, and *philia*.

Eros was commonly associated with the physical aspect of sexual love,[2] although later it acquired philosophical and

[1] Buber, *op. cit.*, p. 15.

[2] This association is evident from the beginning. Both earlier and later forms of the word are used chiefly of sexual passion, either heterosexual or homosexual (see Liddell and Scott, *Greek-English Lexicon*, svv., etc.). The beginnings of love were ascribed to the god Eros, although Aphrodite seems to have presided over the developed relations between men and women, and it was to her that sacrifice was generally offered on the wedding day. Instances of prayer to Eros in connexion with marriage seem to have been rare and only local (e.g. at Boeotian Thespiae, Plutarch, *Amatorius*, 26). He was associated rather with male homosexuality; sacrifice was made to him by the Spartans before going into battle (Athenaeus, *Deipnosoph.*, xiii, 561e).

religious significance. Hence arose the distinction emphasized by Plato[1] between the sensual, 'earthly' *eros* (*pandēmos erōs*) and the 'heavenly' *eros* (*ouranios erōs*), a distinction maintained by Nygren, who opposes to the Christian *agape* the heavenly *eros* 'in its most spiritual and sublimated form'.[2] But however marked the difference between the two forms of *eros*, they have one basic feature in common. In both, the fundamental, essential element is desire—a will-to-possess seeking satisfaction, either on the sensual or on the supersensual plane, in the attainment and enjoyment of its object. This desire is determined entirely by appreciation of a value residing in its object, and with attainment or possession it is fulfilled and ceases.

There is no need to minimize or deprecate the 'selfish' element, the *eros*, in love. If love has any meaning at all, the beloved must be allowed an objective value by reason of which she is sought, and possession of her is desired. Admittedly, in the *I-Thou* of love's relational event she loses this value with the loss of her objective status, but with the inevitable lapse into the condition of a *She* her value returns enhanced, and again awakens the desire which seeks its satisfaction in her. *Eros* therefore is always an indication of the beloved's value, though it is not always the true measure of that value.

Because *eros* ceases with the attainment of its object it might seem that it has no permanent significance in love, but this is not in fact the case. Although not connected exclusively with it, the satisfaction of *eros* belongs most markedly to the sexual life, which alternates between desire and fulfilment—each recurring with never-failing novelty. The *eros* which seeks, either in the sexual life or elsewhere, a once-for-all satisfaction has no place in true love, and belongs to the sphere of passion. For the man and woman who are growing together into an ever-deepening *henosis* there can never be any attainment of

---

[1] *Symposium*, 180D f.   [2] *op. cit.*, i, pp. 33, 133–4, etc.

complete and final satisfaction. The true *eros*, in desiring the beloved physically, desires also and above all the establishment of a permanent and meaningful union in 'one flesh'. In true love there can be an infinite succession of satisfactions, physical and psychical, because of the progressive renewal and intensification of *eros* through perception of an ever-growing value in the beloved. While specially related to the sexual life, *eros* is not bound up exclusively with it, and does not diminish with the passing of sexual desire; it is really directed to the whole person of the beloved, desire for whom is never extinguished in possession since, being always of great worth to the lover, she remains always desirable.

Philia has been defined as a 'mutual relation, a bond which links two centres of consciousness in one'.[1] It is the love of friendship, of mutual giving in which every kind of exchange is comprehended. Not only is there the *philia* which exists between friends—the *philia*, for instance, of David and Jonathan—but there is also the *philia* of the Covenant through which Israel became God's people and He became their God: and *philia* is even involved in the love 'wherewith the Father loved the Son before the foundation of the world, the unity into which all the friends of the Crucified are to be made perfect'.[2] This love stands midway between *eros* and *agape*, and in the relation between man and woman may assume various forms, the most obvious being the bond created by some common interest or concern, which thus forms a basis for their relationship.

Philia is integral to the profound conception of community which finds expression in the union of man and woman as 'one flesh'. Without it, neither *eros* nor *agape* can constitute the basis of an authentic *henosis*; sexual love in its full quality and depth cannot be known if it does not include an experience on every level of all that is meant by a true common life, founded on friendship and mutual exchange. In such a common life, which

[1] John Burnaby, *Amor Dei*, p. 18.   [2] *ibid*.

is the embodiment of the *philia* of lover and beloved, an essential element is freedom. From the beginning they confront one another on terms of unconditional spiritual equality. They grow together first in friendship, and the common life which began in the sharing of interests attains its consummation in the sacramental sharing of one another's bodies; *eros* and *agape* come to enrich and deepen *philia*, not to supersede it.

Agape, neutral in classical Greek, became by New Testament usage a technical term signifying the 'one way relation of which the subject is God and the object man'.[1] This love is neither spontaneous nor emotional. It is an act of will whereby the Christian reproduces the *agape* of Christ—his *agape* is really not his, but the *agape* of Christ realized in him, finding expression through him. As a factor in personal relation *agape* stands in opposition to *eros*, for it is neither evoked nor affected by value of any kind. Hence sexual love, for the Christian, acquires a new quality. The beloved is one for whom Christ died; the lovers are 'in Christ'—incorporated into his mystical Body—and their relation assumes a deeper significance. It is transformed by His *agape* in them, and their love becomes the basis of a union of profound analogical and symbolic meaning. There is not merely an increase of kindliness or benevolence; human standards are transcended, and the beloved is loved for her worth in the sight of God. *Eros* and *philia* are not superseded; they are controlled and enriched by the *agape* which permeates every aspect of the relation.[2]

Nor is 'natural' sexual love radically defective, lacking any altruistic, self-giving element. True, it has been gravely disorganized by sin, and volition in particular has been affected; nevertheless, while reserving for *agape* its special theological meaning, we may not improperly speak of a 'natural' *agape* which is, as it were, the analogue of Christian *agape*. Classical and Hebrew examples are not wanting to

[1] John Burnaby, *Amor Dei*, p. 20; cf. Nygren, *op. cit.*, i, pp. 52–6.
[2] See Otto Piper, *The Christian Interpretation of Sex*, pp. 70 ff.

confirm this. The relation between Christian lovers is simply that of 'natural' love restored and transformed in Christ, and enhanced by the addition of a new quality. *Agape*, therefore, will be used in the following pages to denote, not only the distinctive Christian love, but also the altruistic, self-giving principle inherent in all true love—the activity of the will whereby *eros* is governed and *philia* enriched, and the good of the beloved and of the *henosis* is placed first.

None of the three kinds of love just described is confined solely to one aspect of the love-relation; *eros* cannot be limited to the sphere of sexual activity and the physical relation, for although it is certainly felt very strongly as sexual desire, yet it may also seek mental or spiritual satisfaction from the beloved; *philia* must find, among others, both sexual and religious expression; and *agape* pervades the relation as a whole. Each has its contribution to make to the fulness of love. But balance and proportion between the different constituents of love is not automatic, and is usually attained only with that persistent effort which is one of the joys and responsibilities which lovers share. It is the purpose of *agape* to secure and preserve a due balance by establishing a true objectivity. *Eros* can never be disinterested, and even *philia* by a subtle transformation may become *eros* rationalized or disguised. Without *agape* as the controlling, conditioning, and directing factor, sexual love would be in danger of lapsing into anarchy, and would cease to be a true mode of personal relation.

The *Thou* with whom an *I* enters into relation must be perceived as a *whole* person; distortion of vision precludes true relation, and the real blindness in love (so called) is the failure to see the beloved in her totality. *Eros* never sees her so, and is not 'truly under the sway of the primary word of relation'.[1] As *She* the beloved is continually under valuation; her worth is assessed according to her capacity for affording satisfaction, and she is thus relegated permanently to the world of *It*. In the

[1] Buber, *op. cit.*, p. 16.

purely *erotic* relation she never enters with her lover into the relational event in which objective values are obliterated. Perception and knowledge of the beloved in her totality depend upon the true objectivity of *agape* by which alone she can be seen as she really is, and not upon the false objectivity of *eros* by which she is seen only as her lover wants her to be, and never as a whole person.

This trichotomy of love is not merely academic and theoretical; unfortunately, however, its truth is demonstrated most forcibly in those relations which, by defect or breakdown, show a want of due balance between *eros*, *agape*, and *philia*. Relational failures cannot always or exclusively be attributed to this cause, but it will not infrequently prove to have been contributory if not primary. There are, too, the cases which exhibit a temporary or even permanent disturbance of balance between the three kinds of love sufficient to weaken and impoverish the relation, but not to wreck it. There is a wide margin of safety, but the stage is easily reached at which the lack of balance becomes critical and the whole relation imperilled. Sometimes failure cannot be avoided, but disaster may generally be averted if the nature of the crisis can be recognized in time. Love has a resilience which compensates for the delicacy with which its component elements must be adjusted, and this normally ensures a balance between them sufficient to secure the relation against breakdown. But the disintegrating power of human egocentricity cannot be ignored or trifled with.

It has already been emphasized that *eros*, *philia*, and *agape* have no special or exclusive association, such as *eros* with the physical or *agape* with the spiritual. Erotic and philial love each have their place in every aspect of the total relation, and are overruled and directed by *agape* with reference to that total relation. In every act and every movement of the spirit by which lovers reach out toward one another, *eros*, *agape*, and *philia* are indistinguishably mingled. Relatively, one may

[29]

perhaps be allowed a higher ethical or spiritual value than another, but this implies no gradation in importance. Each love is itself a distinct mode of relation making its own unique and necessary contribution to the total experience, and, without all three in due balance, the relation is defective.

IX

LOVE is inherently tragic. First, there is the tragedy inseparable from the conjunction in love of two free and autonomous persons, and the consequent clash of two wills-to-power. Berdyaev writes of

> . . . an eternal tragic element which has nothing to do with social forms, but is mysteriously and indissolubly connected with death. It would be present if there were only two loving hearts in the world. . . . Pure tragedy arises when two people are completely free, and when a conflict of values takes place between the value of love and the value of freedom or of creative vocation, or of the higher value of the love of God and divine perfection. . . .[1]

Tragedy in this sense belongs inevitably to all human relation. Its intensity in love is simply due to the impulse towards union being stronger there than anywhere else. Two persons, each entirely free, are drawn together in a relation where, sooner or later, each will challenge the other's freedom as it has never been challenged before. Precepts like the 'give and take' of worldly wisdom are meaningless here; the conflict takes place at a level deeper than that with which such platitudes are concerned, and may even pass unperceived. Nor is the conflict simply between two persons in their freedom; it has its counterpart also in the interior struggle in each between

[1] *The Destiny of Man*, p. 200.

the impulse to self-assertion and dominance over the other, and the impulse to complete self-surrender to the other.

If this tragic element can never be absent from human relation, it can at least be modified and even transformed. This is the work of love, which begins from the outset to build up a resistance against all that would imperil or disrupt the union between lover and beloved. With the consummation and the emergence of the new biune organism of the 'one flesh', the nature of the conflict between the self-determining personalities is changed and its acuteness diminishes. Tragedy and tension remain, for the conflict goes on; but at the same time, out of the two separate lives, a *henosis* is being built up at a deeper level than the one on which the conflict occurs. Underneath the superficial clash of wills there is an ever-growing tranquillity of spirit as lover and beloved understand, both before marriage and increasingly afterwards, the truth of their fundamental singleness, and its power against all that makes for disintegration.

There is, next, the tragedy which arises from the fact that when they meet lovers are already members of existing groups or communities. This tragedy is also experienced as tension—this time, not between person and person but between individual and society. It issues from the further fact that something secret to the lovers, something which concerns them alone—that is, their love—is generally attended by consequences which affect the community. For its own sake, therefore, the community must have regard not only to the consequences of love but to love itself. Love, it is true, 'lies outside the social sphere, and has no relation whatever to the community. It is absolutely individual and wholly connected with personality'.[1] Yet it leads to the establishment of the 'one flesh' *henosis*—a new community within the community; it leads usually to procreation (and therefore the continuance of the race) and to the family 'organized in the interests of society

[1] Berdyaev, *op. cit.*, p. 294.

in accordance with the general structure of the community'.[1] Its sexual element may imperceptibly be perverted to immorality or vice, which are agents in racial and social disintegration. Every way the community is deeply concerned with a relation which, paradoxically, is the business of none but the two involved. Thus it happens that 'the most intimate aspect of personality, which simply cannot be judged from outside, and of which the person is shy of speaking to anyone at all, is the most organized and regulated socially'.[2]

Yet always the community remains at the mercy of the individual; the intimate, hidden life of lovers, and their real attitude to one another and to the community, are impenetrable. This affects the Church more than the State. The latter is not at all concerned with the spiritual validity of a love-relation, but only with the necessity of bringing it under the control of society in marriage because of the social consequences involved. For the Church, however, marriage must possess an interior validity which guarantees its conformity to the will of God, and in particular it must have love as its ontological basis. Only the inwardly valid union can possess real significance and constitute a true 'one flesh' *henosis* in the sight of God who looks upon the heart. Yet the Church has no means of ascertaining, for instance, whether one or both of the parties to a marriage upon which she is asked to give the blessing of God are not 'already inwardly united by the bond of love to someone else'.[3] This alone justifies any attempt to bring love within a theological context, and emphasizes the need for instruction to be given by the Church upon the nature and meaning of the premarital as well as the marital relation between man and woman.

Neither community nor Church ordinarily take cognizance of the love-relation until it is known that marriage is intended. But from the moment they exchange their vows, the lovers themselves cannot and must not remain blind to the fact that

---

[1] Berdyaev, *op. cit.*, p. 294.   [2] *ibid.*   [3] See *ibid.*, p. 296.

this intimate, secret love between them must sooner or later inevitably become the concern of the community. It must be with full acceptance of this that they take each other. The situation, which is inescapable yet not of their making, necessarily spells tragedy; they must work out their relation in the face of intrusive social, economic, and family pressures which threaten to disrupt it or bring it into subservience. This is the price of love, for to escape the tension in one form only means encountering it in another and often more acute form. It is easier to accept and conform to the conventions of the community than to rebel against them.

As between the Church, considered as an institution, and its members the position is different; Christians will not wish their relation in love to be other than accordant with God's will. They will seek rather than suffer the blessing of the Church, they will welcome its interest, and will readily accept their new responsibilities within the mystical Body. In Christ all possibility of tension between the lovers and the Divine society is done away. But there will still remain the other tensions, and the inescapable and insoluble paradox that this most intimate thing must become a matter of interest and concern to the community. The situation remains tragic, whether the lovers acquiesce or rebel. And despite the inevitability of this intrusion, there always remains the ironic fact that the community can never satisfy itself that the relation to which it gives its sanction will prove socially beneficial, neither can the Church have any assurance except the assurance of faith, that those upon whom it bestows its approval and blessing will indeed fulfil God's will in their union.

Love is not immune from the tragedy of failure or betrayal. Selfishness or pride can so easily ruin a relation concerning which lofty, not to say extravagant professions have been made. Yet tragedy of this sort is almost of daily occurrence, and those whose lives have been impoverished and outlooks warped as a result are familiar enough. Lovers rightly expect much from

[33]

love, and it is indeed tragic that the cause of breakdown often lies, not in some circumstance beyond their control, but simply in the disintegrating power of unrepented sin.

There is tragedy also in the fact that their love brings men and women to an awareness of certain eternal values. Through the *I-Thou* relation they experience something which stands outside space and time, yet they know, if they are realistic, that their present love is 'not hereafter'—a phrase which implies much more than a mere *carpe diem* attitude. It belongs to this order of things and is inextricably bound up with sex and the physical, which are passing away. Yet it has also a quality which transcends mortality, and through it lovers enter into an awareness of eternity. They feel that the meaning of their experience must be sought, not in the temporal world to which they belong, but in the eternal world upon which a window has now been opened for them. Standing as they seem to do between time and eternity, they are poignantly conscious in the depth of their being of the tension caused by their love. This world is at once familiar, and strange and alien, and there is an ineffable yearning for the other and unattainable world which lies beyond it, into which the lovers may look but cannot enter. There is nothing in this experience which can be explained away in terms of sex and sexual desire; it springs from a purely metaphysical sense of tragedy which cannot be evaded and is, if anything, heightened by release from physical tension. The deeper the love, the stronger is the impulse to attempt an escape from the thralldom of the temporal, and the greater the danger of the false romanticism which speaks of love as 'everlasting' in the wrong sense. To the Christian, however, with his present experience of eternal life in Christ, there will be nothing new or perplexing in this tension.

X

THIS analysis of the sexual love-experience does not pretend to be complete, but enough will have been said both to describe the unique character of the love which is the basis of the 'one flesh' *henosis*, and to show how impossible it is to include all its distinctive features within the limits of a single comprehensive definition.

The different elements in sexual love have only been considered separately for convenience; experimentally they cannot so easily be distinguished. They are generally so synthesized in the immediacy of relation that even their presence may pass undetected, and may be realized only in retrospection. The experience does not depend for its validity upon conscious recognition of its component elements; indeed, the more authentic the love, the less perceptible they will be. With the exception of fidelity, responsibility, and reverence—and, of course, *agape*—they are in no sense willed, but arise out of the event of relational meeting, or out of sexual attraction. Where there is love between a man and a woman every element is present, actually or potentially, and none ever ceases to have significance. This is true even of sexuality in those who are no longer young; being 'one flesh', they can never entirely sever themselves from the intercourse which established their union, maintained and consolidated it, and shaped its character. Hence sexuality becomes an element of permanent significance in their relation. Similarly, though love does not depend upon a perpetual sight of the vision of perfection, it certainly implies its perpetual recollection.

XI

THERE is a common but loose-thinking view of sexual love which associates it almost exclusively with the premarital stage of sexual relation, and so by implication sets it against marriage.

Such an arbitrary and regrettable dichotomy may originate from the mediaeval convention which opposed Courtly Love to marriage, though it is doubtful whether support can be found for this in any continuous tradition. It is, rather, an inference from the apparently loveless character of so many unions, and has been encouraged by the community's concern and interest in the secret and intimate premarital relation between lovers. This relation naturally attracts attention and kindles the imagination to a greater degree than marriage, with its recognized and regulated place in the social structure. There is also the mysterious magnetism of sex itself, which has an interest for the spectator as well as for the lovers, and the element of incalculability which always attends personal encounter and is particularly strong in love. These and other factors combine to stimulate an interest in the premarital relation between men and women which has been attended by unfortunate consequences.

Social tradition, poetry, the novel, the film, and the popular song all agree in treating love as an interesting, exciting, romantic (and, of course, premarital) state, to which is added a piquant element of uncertainty and adventure. The winning and the being won command all attention, diverting it from the more important and significant relation of settled love in marriage, which by contrast is too often treated as commonplace and dull—a fit subject for music-hall witticisms and popular jokes. Many women believe that love only lasts at most for a year after marriage, and that it may not even survive the first month.

For this there is no doubt that the sorry tale of marriage breakdown, and the prosaic or sordid end of many high professions, have largely been responsible. But the result has been to invite concentration upon a less significant, indeed, an almost pre-relational phase of the sexual encounter, at the expense of the love which has reached its consummation in the establishment of the 'one flesh' *henosis*. From the social

standpoint alone this is a serious matter, since emotional insta-
bility and sentimentality are stressed, rather than the quiet and
settled union of husband and wife which means so much to
the community. To this dichotomy may be traced many
marriage failures due to disillusionment, and also the attempts
made from time to time to evolve new forms of sexual relation
as substitutes for marriage, with the implied if not express
intention of safeguarding the primary importance of love.

The only remedy is to assert that from the moment when
lovers accept their vocation to a life as 'one flesh', the love-
experience is one and continuous. Marriage is a specific
relational aspect of sexual love, or, to express it differently, the
premarital and marital relations are in reality only different
modes of the same relation, the latter being the continuation
and development of the former, not something new super-
seding it. The consummation of love in marriage means, not
its termination, but its entry upon another stage, richer and
more significant than the first, yet continuous with it. The
specious but erroneous distinction between love and marriage
is emphasized by the fact that love cannot, like marriage, be
regulated by law, though it may admittedly be controlled by
custom having the coercive force of law. Here the tragic element in love appears. To enter into the relation which has been
analysed and described in the foregoing pages ought to lead by
natural and unhindered stages to the establishment of the *henosis*
and to life as 'one flesh'. Deep down, lovers understand this;
but they do not understand so easily the extent to which
emotion can obscure judgement and prompt wrong choices
which appear to be right ones. Nor do they always appreciate
the extent of their involvement in the life of the community,
and the claim which the community makes upon them.

Ideally, once a true relation in love has been entered and
a man and a woman have accepted their vocation to become
'one flesh', the consummation of that love ought not to have to
depend upon external and intrinsically irrelevant circumstances.

Accepting the human situation as it is, however, the engagement period may serve a useful purpose. Undoubtedly it had
value when convention made it impossible for members of
the different sexes to get to know one another without the
conclusion of some such formal arrangement, and it still has
its use where the compatibility of the couple is not quite
certain, since it affords an opportunity for them to test their
relation in permitted ways, and allows an honourable way out,
approved by society, should it become clear that they were
mistaken. But very often there is no doubt at all. Lovers who
get engaged are generally certain—indeed, the engagement is
the expression of their certainty—and were it not for com-
pliance with convention, submission to economic necessity, or
some other cause irrelevant to their love, would marry forth-
with. Then the engagement is not entered at their own desire;
it is forced upon them under duress, by external pressure. To
attempt to extenuate it by urging the necessity for testing a
mutual compatibility which has already been tested and is not
in doubt comes dangerously near to condoning 'spiritual trial
marriage'. If the engagement is to be justified (as well it may
be) as a time of testing, it ought to begin earlier; as it is, it
generally marks the conclusion of that period, and amounts
simply to a conventional way of announcing a settled intention
to marry at the earliest opportunity. In fact, it will usually be
found that the engagement was entered privately long before
it was made public. But it ought to be recognized that lovers
who are of full age and have made up their minds have a right
to marry, and that it is iniquitous that social or economic
barriers or any other improper hindrance should be interposed
between them and the fulfilment of their vocation to become
'one flesh'. That there have generally been such obstacles, and
that lovers have always accepted them as inevitable, does not
mitigate the tragedy of the situation.

But this criticism of the common attitude towards love
presupposes a serious conception of relation such as lovers

themselves do not always possess. The distinction drawn between the premarital and the marital stages of love tends to encourage irresponsibility and even levity where the former is concerned. Lovers, therefore, must realize that being in love is as serious a matter in one sense as being married. Those who have accepted a vocation to become 'one flesh' are committed already in principle to everything that is implied thereby, even though circumstances may compel them to defer for a time the physical consummation of their union and the realization of that vocation. They are, so to speak, metaphysically 'one flesh'; their relation is no longer casual or experimental, but has something of the high seriousness of the *henosis* to which they have been called but cannot yet enter. This is not to say, of course, that a vocation to marriage may not sometimes be mistaken; in certain cases there may be good cause for a decision to part, but such a decision must never be taken lightly, and it is indeed a grave matter to refuse a vocation which is not in doubt. If engagements were entered in a more responsible spirit, and with a deeper understanding, fewer of them would have to be broken, and fewer marriages would fail. But it is useless to demand that lovers take their relation seriously in the way suggested above, and that the popular distinction between love and marriage be rejected, unless love itself is given theological definition and treated as 'the ontological basis of the marriage union'. Having attempted here to set it in a theological context, we may now pass to a consideration of the 'one flesh' *henosis* in which it finds its highest and most significant expression.

UNION IN 'ONE FLESH'

UNION IN 'ONE FLESH'

I

THE BIBLICAL MEANING
OF 'ONE FLESH'

WHEN Jesus was asked whether divorce is lawful[1] he went behind the Mosaic law with which he had been confronted and appealed to the law of God governing the relations between men and women:

> Therefore shall a man leave his father and his mother, and shall cleave unto his wife: and they shall be one flesh.[2]

St. Paul used the same words, both to explain the analogy between marriage and Christ's union with the Church[3] and to show the momentous consequences which attend even casual or mercenary sexual transactions.[4] These references to Genesis were more than formal citations of a convenient proof-text; they were affirmations of a principle in sexual relation which, although never precisely defined, was clearly held to be of fundamental importance. This principle is expressed in the term 'one flesh', the meaning of which must first be considered.

The emphasis in 'one flesh' is primarily upon the *henosis* which results from the sexual union of man and woman. In Scripture 'one' is a rich and suggestive word. In the Genesis passage it may at first have meant simply that husband and wife become 'one' in relation to the community—that through marriage a new social unit emerges—but when taken into the context of the New Testament it gains greatly in significance.[5]

---

[1] Mark 10.2–12; cf. Matt. 19.3–11.   [2] Gen. 2.24.   [3] Eph. 5.22ff.   [4] I Cor. 6.16.

[5] See the article on *heis* ('one') by Stauffer in the *Theologisches Wörterbuch zum Neuen Testament*, ed. G. Kittel.

It implies the resolution of discord, the transcending of superficial differences and antagonisms at a new and deeper level of existence or experience; not an amalgamation in which the identity of the constituents is swallowed up and lost in an undifferentiated unity, nor a mere conjunction in which no real union is involved. The singleness for which 'one' stands, in its most pregnant use, is organic, not arithmetical, and has a suggestion of uniqueness; it is exemplified at its highest in the mysterious triunity of the one God, of which the biunity of husband and wife is an analogue.

In marriage man and woman become 'one *flesh*'.[1] This means that through the sexual intercourse in which they consummate their love they restore the original pattern of human unity. The older of the two Genesis creation myths describes how God took one of Adam's ribs and built it into a woman.[2] Male and female are thus shown to have a common origin; they are not independent but complementary, and individually incomplete until they have achieved the union in which each integrates and is integrated by the other.

Although the union in 'one flesh' is a physical union established by sexual intercourse (the conjunction of the sexual organs) it involves at the same time the whole being, and affects the personaltiy at the deepest level. It is a union of the entire man and the entire woman. In it they become a new and distinct unity, wholly different from and set over against other human relational unities, such as the family or the race; to bring into existence the 'one flesh' a man must leave his father and his mother. Yet husband and wife in their union remain indissolubly one with all 'flesh'—with the things which are passing away, and this 'fleshly' character of the *henosis* sets

---

[1] In Gen. 2.24 the word is *basar*(=LXX *sarx*), by far the commonest of the Hebrew words in the O.T. denoting 'flesh'. It has a wide range of meaning—the fleshy substance of an animal body (as distinct from the bone, etc.), the body itself, a human being, a blood relation, mankind, any mortal creature, the whole of the transient creation, the sexual organs—between which the LXX differentiates to some extent.

[2] Gen. 2.21f.

a term to its life; it endures until death, but in heaven there is neither marrying nor giving in marriage.

In the following pages these and other aspects of the union between man and woman in 'one flesh' will be examined in more detail.

II

'ONE FLESH' AND MARRIAGE

CHRISTIAN theology, remarkably enough, has taken little account of the important Biblical idea of 'one flesh', and has generally treated it as synonymous with marriage, in terms of which the legitimate sexual relation between man and woman has nearly always been described. This neglect, and the confusion which has arisen in consequence, was due to ignorance of the inner meaning of sexual union, and to failure on that account to discriminate clearly between the institutional and the ontological aspects of marriage. For this, there were historical reasons:

> The Christian Church for many centuries simply accepted and conformed to the Roman law and Roman customs so far as was compatible with Christian views, commonly confirming the union by religious benedictions.[1]

Inevitably marriage came to be regarded principally from the institutional and legal standpoint, and Canon law was in many respects indebted to the Civil law. For instance:

> The dictum of Ulpian, *nuptias non concubitus sed consensus facit* (consent, not cohabitation makes a marriage), became accepted as an axiom of the Church's law . . .[2]

[1] O. D. Watkins, *Holy Matrimony*, p. 78.
[2] A. T. Macmillan, *What is Christian Marriage?*, p. 69; cf. *Summa Theol.*, III Supp. xlv, 1, 2 *resp.* and 4 *resp:* marriage is a union between one man and one woman effected by mutual verbal consent expressive of the inward intention of the parties, and without that consent no union is valid.

with the result that attention was never sufficiently directed to the fact that sexual intercourse alone establishes the 'one flesh' union. It is, of course, true that consent is integral to marriage, but it cannot by itself effect any *henosis* such as 'one flesh' implies.

Into the rigid framework of this legal, institutional view of marriage which became dominant in the Church both theology and relational ideals were forced, and every tendency of thought which might conflict with its basic assumptions was precluded. This is not to say that those basic assumptions were wholly wrong, but they needed adjustment and modification in the light of the principles of sexual relation and union declared in Scripture. Of those principles, however, little account was taken, and theologians became engrossed in the institutional aspect of marriage at the expense of its interior, ontological aspect. The former, of course, has its importance, and must be of increasing consequence as the Church endeavours to maintain its witness in the midst of a secular society, for it is through the institution of Christian marriage that its distinctive teaching about sexual union is proclaimed. But behind the institution, giving it validity and determining its character, lies a theology which must be grounded in the Biblical idea of 'one flesh'.

'One flesh', therefore, denotes the essential informing principle in marriage, the interior, ontological aspect of sexual union. Every true institutional marriage is simply an embodiment or formal expression of the mysterious *henosis* established by man and woman in the consummation of their love. Between marriage and 'one flesh' there is, and can be, no antagonism; they are distinct but not independent, inseparable but not synonymous, and only appear as conflicting concepts when attention is concentrated (as it has been in the past) upon the legal, institutional aspect of marriage to the virtual exclusion of the ontological. Then confusion and erroneous conclusions are bound to ensue. For instance, acceptance of

the axiom *nuptias non concubitus sed consensus facit* (a principle correct so far as it went) had the effect of obscuring the tremendous implications of St. Paul's assertion[1] that sexual intercourse (which may involve a kind of 'consent' to which social, legal, or ecclesiastical recognition cannot be given) establishes a state of 'one flesh'—thus leading the Schoolmen to deny that the sexual act is of the essence of marriage.[2] Any attempt, therefore, to reinstate the principle of 'one flesh' is bound to appear as a challenge to certain traditional assumptions concerning marriage, though it will not be difficult to show that no lowering, much less abandonment of Christian standards is implied, but rather, the setting forth of a new and lofty relational ideal. In redressing the balance upset by a disproportionate emphasis upon marriage as an institution it is necessary to direct attention specially to the significance of union in 'one flesh', but this does not mean going to the other extreme. We are concerned here simply with an examination of the essential character of the relation into which God calls men and women for His glory and their good, fully recognizing the importance of the institutional forms in which that relation finds expression.

III

THE ESTABLISHMENT OF THE 'ONE FLESH' UNION BY SEXUAL INTERCOURSE

FOLLOWING Roman law, the Church has always taught that the essential constitutive factor in marriage is the consent of the parties, and not their sexual union. Augustine only gives qualified approval to irregular unions where the intention of

[1] Cf. I Cor. 6.16.
[2] See Macmillan, *op. cit.*, p. 73; cf. *Summa Theol.*, III Supp. lviii, 1 ad 1; li, 1 ad 4.

the man and the woman can be held to imply a real element of consent to a relation in almost every respect equivalent to marriage.[1] While they generally recognized sexual intercourse as an essential feature of marriage, none of the Fathers regarded it as the means whereby alone the union of husband and wife is established, or a state of 'one flesh' set up.[2] The Schoolmen likewise insisted that *consensus facit matrimonium*, though according to Peter Lombard there were different opinions as to what this meant; some held that after the exchange of vows at betrothal *sponsus* and *sponsa* were truly married (*veri conjuges*), others, that marriage proper followed upon intercourse and that the betrothed were not *conjuges* until after the *commixtio sexus*.[3] In the *Summa Theologica* it is stated that although the union of the sexes is ordained for carnal intercourse, only the ability to fulfil the marriage act is requisite, and not its performance, since it does not effect, and is not necessary to a marriage.[4] Therefore the union of Joseph and Mary, although unconsummated, was a true marriage in its first perfection or formal essence,[5] but not in its second perfection or the operation by which it attains its end, since

> . . . both consented to the nuptial bond, but not expressly to the bond of the flesh, save on the condition that it was pleasing to God.[6]

Nevertheless, it was generally allowed that sexual intercourse was integral to marriage and that the contract between *sponsus*

---

[1] *de bono conj.* 5 (v).

[2] Statements such as . . . *postquam copulatione conjugii viri atque mulieris unum corpus efficitur* . . . (Gregory the Great, *Epist.* xi. 50) and [*Deus docet*] *nos, cum duo inter se corpora fuerint copulata, unum corpus efficere* (Lactantius, *Inst.* vi. 23) appear to refer simply to union in marriage, and not specifically to sexual intercourse.

[3] *Sent.*, lib. IV dist. xxvii. 5 and 6.

[4] III Supp. xlviii 1 *resp.*; lviii 1 ad 1; li 1 ad 4. Sexual intercourse following betrothal, however, is held to effect a marriage unless there is clear evidence of fraud or deceit, *ibid.*, xlvi 2 *resp.*; cf. xli 4.

[5] 'A certain inseparable union of souls, by which husband and wife are pledged by a bond of mutual affection that cannot be sundered', *Summa Theol.*, III xxix 2 *resp.*; cf. *ibid.*, III Supp. xlii 4 ad 2.

[6] *ibid.*, III xxix 2 *resp.*; cf. Augustine, *Hom. in N.T.* I. xiii (21), etc.

and *sponsa* expressed in their mutual consent was completed by the consummation.

The consent by which marriage was held to be constituted had to be

> . . . free, mutual, directed to marriage as understood by the Church, and intended to be immediately operative.[1]

But it can hardly be maintained that all or even most marriages, especially in earlier times and among the ruling and noble classes, fulfilled the spirit or even the letter of this requirement. Theoretically mutual consent was necessary, but it is well-known that in very many cases the bride's was virtually extorted from her, since she had no option but to comply with the wishes and arrangements of her parents or guardians.[2] It is farcical to pretend that the 'consent' so given was that envisaged by the theologians and canonists; whatever its formal validity, its inward validity is seriously in doubt. If true marriage is effected only by consent as defined above, there have been many unions which cannot be termed true marriages.[3]

In determining the constitutive factor in marriage, however, there is no need to oppose intercourse to consent; like the institutional and ontological aspects of sexual union, they are really complementary. Consent is the basis of the public exchange of vows which expresses the intention of the parties and provides the only satisfactory *terminus a quo* for the recognition of their union by the community; it may therefore properly be said to effect marriage on the institutional level. But the mere exchange of vows, whether in public or in private,

---

[1] Macmillan, *op. cit.*, p. 71.

[2] See C. S. Lewis, *op. cit.*, p. 13.

[3] A marriage was, of course, theoretically invalidated if consent had been secured by force (*vis*), fear (*metus*), or abduction (*raptus*), but such diriment impediments could rarely be alleged by or on behalf of the bride concerned, since satisfactory proof was difficult or impossible to get. Recourse was sometimes had to such impediments, however, to procure the dissolution of a marriage which the husband no longer desired to continue.

does not and cannot bring about any essential change in the character of the personal relation between man and woman. That is to say, consent by itself has no ontological connexion with marriage and is powerless to effect a union in 'one flesh'; it is simply the precondition of the establishment of that union by sexual intercourse.

Not *every* sexual act, however, sets up a valid *henosis*, but only that which is done under conditions implying consent as it has usually been understood—consent, not merely to an act of intercourse, but to everything that follows from it.[1] Mutual consent, therefore, is in fact fundamental, as Christian tradition has always insisted—but it is fundamental, not because by itself it effects an ontological change in the relation between a man and a woman by uniting them in the unique, mysterious *henosis* of 'one flesh', but because it is essentially prerequisite to the sexual intercourse by which that *henosis* is established. This important distinction has not been appreciated simply because marriage has always been viewed institutionally rather than ontologically.

At this point a difficulty must be faced. If sexual intercourse is so significant an act, and is attended by such momentous consequences, what are we to make of St. Paul's assertion:

Know ye not that he that is joined to a harlot is one body? For, the twain, saith he, shall become one flesh.[2]

Is there not a radical contradiction in the statement that even the most irresponsible and ephemeral connexion between a man and a woman (whether in ignorance or defiance of the consequences) makes them, like husband and wife, 'one flesh'? In fornication every condition necessary for the establishment of a true *henosis* is absent; there is consent, perhaps, but it is directed to a wrong end; there is certainly no love, apart from a perverted *eros*; there is no intention of fidelity, no making

---

[1] Cf. again Augustine, *de bono conj.* 5 (v).   [2] I Cor. 6.16.

and sharing of a common life, no recognition of any responsibility to the community—yet 'he that is joined to a harlot is one body [with her]'. The fact that St. Paul's assertion has received little attention from commentators in the past suggests that it has generally been found a hard saying, though it is clearly integral to his argument at that point, and cannot be dismissed as a reckless *obiter dictum*. It will be worth while, therefore, to pause here and review the discussion in I Cor. 6.12–20.

St. Paul contrasts two kinds of union. There is, first, that of the believer with Christ, expressed in the metaphor of the body and its members—a spiritual, metaphysical union analogically exemplified in the true *henosis* of husband and wife: 'he that is joined unto the Lord is one spirit'. Second, there is union with a harlot—a parody of the true *henosis* and so of the marriage between the heavenly Bridegroom and his Bride. St. Paul, therefore, can set before the Corinthians two alternatives; union with Christ or union with a prostitute. The Christian who has intercourse with a harlot becomes thereby a member, so to speak, of the Devil's community; this shocking travesty of the 'one flesh' union is the analogue of the 'marriage' between the Evil One and those who have surrendered their lives to him. Fornication cuts off the believer from both the faithful and their Lord: '. . . shall I then take away the members of Christ, and make them members of a harlot?' The whole argument turns upon the fact that sexual intercourse, whether licit or illicit, has one inevitable consequence; therefore it is not really contradictory to say that 'he that is joined to a harlot is one body [with her]'.

His use of 'body' (*sōma*) instead of 'flesh' (*sarx*) shows how well St. Paul understood the significance of sexual union. The 'body' is not simply the physical organism, but the total self; 'one flesh' and 'one body' are synonymous. Intercourse therefore is much more than a mere physical act which takes place on the periphery, as it were, of personal experience; it involves

and affects the whole man and the whole woman in the very centre and depth of their being, so that afterwards neither can ever be as if they had never come together. This is true even of fornication, which cannot be excused or dismissed as something insignificant, done in complete detachment, and from which no consequences follow. Thus the verbal substitution serves both to reveal the true character of sexual union, and to expose the fallacy, as common now as it was among the Corinthians, that casual and promiscuous intercourse is 'natural' and means nothing.

But while we allow, with St. Paul, that sexual intercourse always establishes a 'one flesh' union, it is clear that in every case the character of the union will be determined by the character of its constitutive act. Thus a distinction may be drawn between two sharply contrasted states of 'one flesh':

1. The true, authentic *henosis* is effected by intercourse following consent between a man and a woman who love one another and who act freely, deliberately, responsibly, and with the knowledge and approval of the community, and in so doing (whether they know it or not) conform to the Divine law. In this class must also be included unions of the kind described by Augustine in *de bono conjugali* 5 (v), which lack nothing but public recognition.
2. The false, invalid 'one flesh' union is effected by casual or mercenary acts of fornication, or by adultery.

It would seem desirable to add to these a third category:

3. There are very many unions which appear to be valid, but which must properly be termed defective. These are the marriages which have no foundation in love, as it has been described in this study, or which, because of sexual or psychical maladjustment, represent a level of personal relation which falls considerably below the ideal implied by 'one flesh'.

There are cases, however, such as rape and the seduction of the young or the feeble-minded, where it would be absurd to press the application of St. Paul's principle; it was clearly never intended to apply to them, and it is certain that the mere occurrence of the sexual act without consent, desire or understanding cannot be held to make two persons 'one body'. But whenever a man and a woman enter freely into sexual relation, the principle holds good; their intercourse always makes them in some sense 'one flesh', and where the union is false and invalid its redemption in marriage is possible through the growth of love and responsibility.

Sexual intercourse is an act of the whole self which affects the whole self; it is a personal encounter between man and woman in which each does something to the other, for good or for ill, which can never be obliterated. This remains true even when they are ignorant of the radical character of their act. It cannot, therefore, be treated simply as sensual indulgence. Fornication is more than an isolated, pleasurable exercise of the sexual organs; it is the expression of an attitude of mind in which God, other persons, and the self are all involved. But sexual intercourse, although an act in which the whole man and the whole woman engage, is nevertheless without meaning unless it consummates a true love and expresses their acceptance and affirmation of the consequent ontological change in themselves and their relation. That is to say, their intention and the context of their intercourse determine the character both of the act itself and of the resultant state of 'one flesh'. In their coming together they either affirm or deny all that sexual intercourse means. In the one case they become knit together in a mysterious and significant *henosis* and fulfil their love as husband and wife; in the other they merely enact a hollow, ephemeral, diabolical parody of marriage which works disintegration in the personality and leaves behind a deeply-seated sense of frustration and dissatisfaction—though this may never be brought to the surface of consciousness and

[53]

realized. So profound, however, are the consequences of sexual intercourse that they can only be adequately expressed by saying that every act initiates or maintains a state of 'one flesh' which either affirms or negates its own inner meaning. In this sense sexual union is more significant for marriage than consent, and is the criterion with reference to which the character of all sexual relation must be estimated.

IV

THE SIGNIFICANCE OF SEX AND SEXUAL UNION

St. Paul, as we have seen, had a profound understanding of the significance of sexual intercourse as an act of the total self by which a union in 'one flesh' is initiated. The steps by which the Church, during the first six centuries of its history, gradually lost its hold upon this and other Biblical insights into sex and marriage, and became committed to views which were often unscriptural, negative, and repressive, demand more extensive consideration than is possible in this study. A brief summary, therefore, and a reference to mediaeval developments, must suffice at this point by way of introduction to an examination of the place of sexuality in the life of husband and wife as 'one flesh'.

A noticeable feature of Patristic thought, particularly in the West, is the growing suspicion (indeed, it amounts to fear) of sex, which attains extravagant, even ridiculous proportions in the writings of Tertullian and Jerome, and relapses into a more moderate but negative attitude in those of Augustine, Ambrose, and Gregory the Great. In the view of these latter,

1. in some sense never clearly defined, the principle of sin was particularly inherent in sexuality;

2. sexual intercourse was
> (a) not sinful (that is, 'excused') when directed exclusively and deliberately to procreation,
>
> (b) venially sinful when used by husband and wife for the relief of incontinence,
>
> (c) otherwise sinful, whatever its motive or occasion—though in what precise degree, there was a difference of opinion;

3. sexual pleasure was always and under all circumstances sinful, though it would have been excused, presumably, if incidental to procreation, and would have been regarded only as venially faulty if incidental to the relief of incontinence.

The significance of sex in the personal life of the individual was never appreciated, nor was sexual intercourse seen to possess any meaning or even importance in the experience of husband and wife as 'one flesh', save for the purpose of procreation.

Thus early Christianity left to succeeding ages an unbalanced conception of sex and sexual intercourse, and an entirely mistaken view of sexual pleasure. While in theory the seat of sexual sin was held to reside in the will and not in sexuality itself, the distinction was rarely and inconsistently observed. This failure to understand sex contributed to the exaltation of celibacy, which in its turn deprived most of the Western clergy and theologians of the experience which would have given them, as married men, a more sympathetic approach to the subject. There were also other reasons for the prevalent attitude:

1. certain ideas relative to the connexion between sex, sin, and evil had been inherited by Christianity from Judaism;[1]

[1] See N. P. Williams, *The Ideas of the Fall and of Original Sin.*

2. a mistaken and exaggerated view of virginity and its merits had become established in the West (the East was in certain respects more liberal and moderate);

3. Oriental dualistic theories had evoked a sympathetic response in some Christian circles, whence their influence infiltrated into the Church at large;

4. ascetic ideals, some of them perhaps derived from ethnic sources, exerted a very strong appeal in several directions;

5. by no means least, there was a vigorous reaction from pagan licentiousness; rigid disciplinary restrictions were necessary, and a certain 'puritanism' inevitable, when converts had daily to witness the practice of immoralities from which they had only lately been saved, and into which there was a constant temptation to relapse.

Nevertheless it is remarkable that the Fathers should have failed so completely to appreciate the bearing upon sex of the doctrines of Creation and the Incarnation, and that the moral degradation of their times did not impel them to attempt a Christian theory of sex based upon the truth which they recognized in the abstract—the goodness and God-givenness of those faculties which the heathen abused.

Scholastic thought, by contrast, was moderate. The view that the sexual act, *per se*, is somehow sinful or guilty was first modified under the influence of the Augustinian theory that it is fully excused by the *bona matrimonii*, and then abandoned in favour of the idea that although in some sense evil, it is not morally evil. While sex itself was acquitted of any inherent taint, every concrete act of intercourse since the Fall contained this element of evil, but opinion was divided as to its location. Hugo of St. Victor thought that it lay in the pleasure concomitant with the act; Peter Lombard, that it was connected with sexual desire; Albertus Magnus, that it was to be found

in the weakness of man's reason, whereby he cannot enjoy pleasure without losing sight of the First Good. St. Thomas, who 'deepens and subtilizes' the last view, traced it to the *ligamentum rationis* or 'submergence of the rational faculty' which accompanies the desire and pleasure.[1] Sexual enjoyment is not morally evil if it is according to reason, and 'reason itself demands that the use of reason be interrupted at times': hence in itself it is not sinful, though it proceeds from the sin of our first parents, since in Paradise no pleasure, however intense, would have deflected the mind from its concentration upon the First Good.[2] But if pleasure is the chief end for which married persons come together, and is not merely incidental to procreation, their intercourse is venially sinful, while if a man is 'too ardent a lover of his wife', so that 'his ardour carries him away from the goods of marriage', he commits mortal sin;[3] all passionate love between husband and wife is excluded. Not only is the sexual act unessential in marriage, but marriage without it is holier[4]—a mediaeval survival of the spirit of primitive syneisaktism. Nevertheless, the marriage blessings sufficiently excuse intercourse,[5] which is in fact meritorious when it takes place between the husband and wife who are in a state of grace with the motive either of justice (the discharge of the marriage debt) or of religion (the procreation of children to worship God), and only venially sinful if the motive is lust, but not so as to exclude the *bona matrimonii*; otherwise, however, it is always mortally sinful.[6]

While the Scholastic view, as epitomized in the Supplement

[1] C. S. Lewis, *op. cit.*, p. 16; see the discussion and references on pp. 15–17.

[2] *Summa Theol.*, I–II xxxiv 1 ad 1.; this view, says Dr. Lewis, 'may suggest to us something much less like the purity of Adam in Paradise than the cold sensuality of Tiberius in Capri', *ibid.*, p. 17.

[3] *Summa Theol.*, III Supp. xlix 6 *resp.*; cf. Peter Lombard's quotation with approval of a saying, *omnis ardentior amator propriae uxoris, adulter est*, *Sent.*, lib. iv, Dist. xxxi 6.

[4] *Summa Theol.*, III Supp. xlii 4 *sed cont.*, cited from Peter Lombard, *Sent.*, lib. iv Dist. xxvi 7; cf. *Summa Theol.*, III xxix 2.

[5] *Summa Theol.*, III Supp. xlix 4 *resp.*, 5 *resp.*

[6] *ibid.*, xli 4 *resp.*

to Part III of the *Summa Theologica*, represents in some respects a considerable advance upon that of most of the Western Fathers, it suffers from the same failure to attempt an assessment of sex and sexual intercourse in terms of personality and personal relation, and the entire approach of the Schoolmen to the subject, divorced as it was from experience, is inevitably academic and defective in understanding. It is profoundly true that a man can only know the meaning of sex through the act of 'knowing' a woman. In this respect most Anglican theologians of the Reformation and Caroline periods were at an advantage, having judged that marriage would serve better to godliness, though they were still fettered by a conservatism which maintained with but little modification much of the Augustinian tradition which had held the field for more than a millennium. Nevertheless, Anglicanism affords evidence of a new and deeper understanding of sexual union such as could not but result from the changed attitude to marriage reflected in passages like those quoted from Becon and Taylor in Part I of this study—though it must be allowed that what seem to be fresh insights were sometimes only the unintentional by-products of anti-Roman polemic. Perhaps the most interesting of the comparatively few express references to the sexual act occurs in Taylor's *Holy Living*:

. . . although in this [act], as in eating and drinking, there is an appetite to be satisfied, which cannot be done without pleasing that desire; yet since that desire and satisfaction was intended by nature for other ends, they should never be separated from those ends, but always be joined *with all or one* of these ends, with a desire of children, or to avoid fornication, or to lighten and ease the cares and sadnesses of household affairs, or to endear each other; but never with a purpose, either in act or desire, to separate the sensuality from those ends which hallow it.[1]

[1] *Works* (1847), iii, p. 63. (My italics.)

Here he seems to allow that intercourse has other legitimate ends than offspring, and that husband and wife may properly come together with other intentions than procreation.

This cursory survey could have been expanded considerably without bringing to light further material bearing upon the significance of sexual union. That it could have any significance at all in itself and in terms of personality would have been incredible to the divines of past ages. Within marriage the sexual act was a procreative mechanism which also served as a means of relief for the incontinent, but that is all; there is no hint that it had a meaning beyond the limited purpose it was held to fulfil. This was without doubt the result of what Dr. E. C. Messenger has called the 'deformation of the Christian Tradition' by Gnostic and Manichaean influences,[1] and its consequences have in fact been more destructive and far-reaching than he allows. In attempting, therefore, to work out a Christian theology of sex there are few authorities to whom appeal can be made, and allowance is necessary for the fact that not a little in the tradition which has descended to us is misleading and untrue to fundamental Biblical insights and principles. To these handicaps the reader will perhaps charitably ascribe at least some of the shortcomings in the following consideration of the significance of sexual union in the life of husband and wife.

In the first place it must be emphasized that sex is one of God's gifts to man and woman, and as such is good in itself and to be 'received with thanksgiving'; there is no place for the unconsciously blasphemous attitude which regards sexual activity as something 'nasty' or 'impure'. On the contrary, the right use of the sexual faculties is one of the most natural ways by which God is glorified in the body. This, however, demands a Godward orientation of the will; in the immediacy of intercourse there can be consciousness of none but the

[1] *The Mystery of Sex and Marriage in Catholic Theology* (*Two in One Flesh*, Part II), p. 142.

beloved, but the act itself must take place in the context of a common God-centred life and must be offered to Him—in intention beforehand, in thanksgiving afterwards—as husband and wife silently acknowledge the Author of their love. The fate of Paolo and Francesca[1] stands as a warning to all who deliberately allow 'the prolongation of the self-indulged moment':[2] it is nothing less than separation from God for ever—'the Now of heaven without heaven'—and it is to this that Francesca refers when she speaks of Paolo as 'he who shall never be divided from me'.[3]

Reference has already been made[4] to the need felt by lovers for some means of communication more adequate than speech. There comes a time when words fail and the tongue cannot utter what is in the heart; yet expression of some kind is an imperative necessity—indeed, without it a personal relation like that of man and woman in 'one flesh' cannot continue. Part of the importance of sexual intercourse is that it affords husband and wife a medium for those mutual disclosures for which no words can be found; the senses become the channel of communication for all that lies too deep for utterance and yet must somehow be told. Such intercourse is necessarily pleasurable because of what is expressed, and not merely because it is a means of sensual gratification. There is no doubt that the theological suspicion of sexual pleasure already mentioned has been partly responsible for the fact that this important aspect of intercourse has not been appreciated.

If God is to be glorified and love expressed through the sexual act there must be some understanding of what is known as sexual 'technique'. The term itself is perhaps unfortunate, implying as it seems to do either formalism or calculated sensuality in intercourse, but it is difficult to suggest a better. To attain a sufficient command of his instrument or medium the musician or painter has to acquire a technique, and it

---

[1] Dante, *Inferno*, V. 73–142; see Charles Williams, *Religion and Love in Dante*, pp. 19–20, and *The Figure of Beatrice*, p. 127.
[2] *Religion and Love in Dante*, p. 20.　　[3] *Inferno*, V. 135.　　[4] See Part, I, § VI.

cannot be supposed that husband and wife will be able to express themselves or use their sexual gifts aright unless they understand their own bodies. It is still widely thought that instinct is a sufficient and reliable guide, but this is not so; ignorance, clumsiness, or want of sympathy can have devastating consequences, and all who intend marriage have a positive duty to acquire an adequate knowledge of sexual technique. Here we are not concerned with the details involved; these can easily be studied in one of the many books available on this subject. But it will not be out of place to urge that during their engagement lovers ought to think about and discuss their attitude to this side of the relation they are shortly to enter, frankly sharing both their knowledge and their ignorance, so that they may help and teach one another, and learn to look forward without apprehension or embarrassment to the intercourse in which they will consummate their love and build up together their common life as 'one flesh'.

Ideally the essential quality of this life should be revealed to husband and wife through the sexual act, but this does not always happen. Not infrequently they are aware that their intercourse lacks the meaning it should possess, that it fails somehow to express even what is most memorable and authentic in their own experience. This is because it confronts them simultaneously with the quality of the relational ideal which they are called to realize, and with the quality of the common life which they are actually living; every sexual act is at once an accurate reflection of, and a judgement upon, their whole relation. Any incompatibility between the ideal and the actual is experienced as a tension which disturbs their intercourse and indicates that they are failing to work out satisfactorily in the life of every day all that 'one flesh' implies. They must therefore pay careful heed to the quality of their relation as it is made known to them in their coming together, for the sexual act will always be either a joyful affirmation of their common life, or a revelation of its defects.

Lastly, through sexual intercourse man and woman come to understand the meaning of their masculinity and femininity, and discover the solution to the enigma of personal existence: Why am I a man? Why am I a woman? To these questions they can give no answer themselves; they only know that it must be sought in sexual experience, and they cannot rest until they have found it. That is why, during adolescence, there is often an acute and sometimes distressing awareness of sex, which needs careful, sympathetic handling. There is no short cut to the answer; only through the sexual act in the context of the 'one flesh' *henosis* can a man, as husband, reveal to a woman the secret of her womanhood, and a woman, as wife, reveal to a man the secret of his manhood.[1]

This explains why the Biblical term for sexual intercourse is generally 'to know'. It is used indiscriminately in Scripture for all kinds of sexual relation,[2] and is certainly no mere euphemism. Although it has a wide range of reference it is clearly, like 'one flesh', an ambivalent term which attains its full significance only when used of the intercourse between husband and wife, who in 'knowing' one another also come to know themselves and the meaning of the mystery of sex. It is, says Dr. Piper,

> . . . obviously only comprehensible if, while it draws a veil, it gives expression to an essential element of sex. . . . The use of the term 'to know' in connexion with sex life does not imply that from the standpoint of the Bible all knowledge is sexually conditioned, but sexual knowledge is certainly regarded by the Bible as the exemplar of true knowledge.[3]

[1] For a larger treatment of this subject, see Otto Piper, *The Christian Interpretation of Sex*, pp. 52–67; also his essay, *The Christian in the Sexual Disorder of the Present Day* in *Education for Christian Marriage*, esp. pp. 39–41 and 50–1.

[2] Between husband and wife, e.g. Gen. 6.1, 17, 25; I Sam 1.19; cf. Matt. 1.25; with a prostitute, Gen. 38.26; of rape, Judg. 19.25; and even of homosexuality, Gen. 19.5. It is used of woman as well as of men: see Gen. 19.8; Judg. 11.39; etc.

[3] *The Christian Interpretation of Sex*, pp. 52–3.

Having considered briefly the sexual aspect of life as 'one flesh', one important question remains: When and how often ought intercourse to take place? St. Paul's injunction is well known:

> Defraud ye not one the other, except it be by consent for a season, that ye may give yourselves unto prayer, and may be together again, that Satan tempt you not because of your incontinency.[1]

though he makes it clear that it is given 'by way of permission, not of commandment'; nevertheless he understands intercourse as a duty owed by the married to one another:

> Let the husband render unto the wife her due: and likewise also the wife unto the husband.[2]

To refrain, except temporarily by mutual agreement, after the manner of a fast, is to deprive the partner in marriage of a benefit to which he or she is entitled. St. Paul here is simply anxious about the consequences of unwise asceticism, but his words contain more truth than he realized. The sexual act plays an important part in the upbuilding and consolidation of the *henosis*, and there must be good reason for its intermission beyond a reasonable length of time; abstinence which causes frustration and exposes the weaker or less willing partner to temptation defeats its own end.

Neither St. Paul nor later writers, however, say anything about the normal frequency of intercourse; in early and mediaeval times the theologians of the Church were more concerned to lay down occasions for abstinence. Thus the sexual act was forbidden during pregnancy by many of the Fathers;[3] Jerome condemns those who communicate on the day they have had sexual relations;[4] Gregory the Great would deny participation in the great feasts to those who had lain

[1] I Cor. 7.5. [2] *ibid.*, 7.3.
[3] See Messenger, *op. cit.*, Part II, p. 152, for examples. [4] *Epist.* xxii,22.

with their wives the night before;[1] candidates for baptism abstained from the use of marriage;[2] and two sixth-century regulations[3] refuse intercourse for a time to the newly-baptized (classing it with 'luxurious feasts' and the theatre) and require the newly-married to abstain on the night of the wedding. St. Thomas Aquinas also deprecates sexual relations on feast days,[4] and deferment of the consummation of a marriage for three nights after the ceremony was held by some to be binding in conscience. Pope Pius X, however, condemned as 'rigorism' the view that the married ought not to communicate immediately after intercourse,[5] and Dr. Messenger says:

> Indeed, in itself, it would seem essentially right and proper that those who have, by joining themselves to each other in the sex act, given, as it were, a sacramental illustration of the union between Christ and the Church, should proceed as soon as possible to receive the real Sacrament of Unity, whereby Christ unites himself to our souls, and ourselves to Him, in such a way that we become 'members of His body, of His flesh and of His bones'.[6]

The Anglican Reformers and their successors had, of course, already repudiated the early and mediaeval restrictions on intercourse. Jewel, for instance, held that St. Paul enjoined abstinence only on extraordinary occasions; it was to be, not for the purpose of private devotion, but for

> ... the general and solemn prayer of the whole congregation which then [in the Apostles' time], as in times of persecution and fear of enemies, was kept only in the night.[7]

[1] *Dial.*, i.10.
[2] Augustine, *de fid. et op.*, viii; Ambrose, *de Elia*, lxxix.
[3] *Statuta ecclesiae antiqua*, 24 and 101.
[4] *Summa Theol.*, III Supp. lxiv 7, 8 and 9.
[5] See Messenger, *op. cit.*, Part I (*Introduction to Sex and Marriage*), p. 9; Part III (*The Practice of Sex and Marriage*), p. 24.
[6] *op. cit.*, Part III, p. 32.
[7] *Defence of the Apology of the Church of England*, Part II, *Works* (Parker Society), iii, p. 404.

Jeremy Taylor also denounces enforced abstention from the sexual act on the wedding night, before Communion, and during Lent.[1]

Two distinct considerations govern the frequency of intercourse. First, there is the fact that man's life is a life set in a temporal context; his waking hours, passed between one 'death' of sleep and the next, are symbolic of his whole existence, and the day is his natural unit of time. Repeated daily acts, therefore, are sacramental expressions of abiding truth, for his most significant affirmations need to be made again and again—hence the celebration of the Eucharist morning by morning; the once-for-all sacrifice must be continually re-presented. So Dr. Herbert Doms says:

The human spirit can never communicate itself adequately in a single act.[2]

and

a human being cannot be consummated in a single act, but only in acts repeated throughout the course of his life.[3]

Something so meaningful as sexual intercourse demands regular repetition, and its frequency must be determined by other than biological factors alone. It is the sacramental expression of the *henosis* of husband and wife, the means by which they are confirmed in their union and the 'one flesh' is nourished and built up. This does not, of course, necessarily require the daily performance of the sexual act (though it does not preclude it), since other considerations are also involved.

This brings us to the second point—the importance of the personal element. It should be recognized that, generally speaking, there is no such thing as normal or abnormal frequency, and many factors will combine to determine when and how often intercourse occurs. Individuals differ widely

[1] *Ductor Dubitantium*, III, iv, § 13; *Works*, x (1852), p. 414.
[2] *The Meaning of Marriage*, p. 24.   [3] *ibid.*, p. 53.

in their needs and temperament, and account must be taken of age, bodily health, state of mind, habit of life, and various kinds of sexual periodicity. Generalization is thus impossible and mutual understanding between husband and wife the more necessary in consequence, but it is proper nevertheless to insist that intercourse of reasonable frequency is integral to their life as 'one flesh', due regard being paid to the special circumstances of each marriage.

An androcentric social tradition established a one-sided interpretation of the idea of the *debitum* or marriage debt, and in some places and among certain classes the distinction between the husband's 'rights' and the wife's 'duties' still survives. The notion that the husband is entitled to intercourse and that, regardless of her personal feelings, the wife ought to comply with his wishes, was undoubtedly encouraged by the absurd but prevalent belief that during coition the woman is passive, and that for her to derive any pleasure from the act is indecent. The bride's promise in the Marriage Service to 'obey' her husband was often understood as an implicit undertaking to submit to his sexual demands. Fortunately, education has largely dispelled such ideas. Scripture knows nothing of this crude conception of *debitum* and St. Paul makes it clear that in marriage rights and duties are mutual:

> Let the husband render unto the wife her due: and likewise also the wife unto the husband. The wife hath not power over her own body, but the husband: and likewise also the husband hath not power over his own body, but the wife. Defraud ye not one the other. . . .[1]

Life as 'one flesh' means surrender of one's body to the other, in return for which one receives the responsibility of 'power' over the other's body. It is obvious how this principle applies to the husband, but it is not always understood that it applies

[1] I Cor. 7.3-5.

equally to the wife; only in special circumstances, for instance, may she refuse a reasonable request for intercourse. Neither of them, however, should think of this matter in terms of rights and duties alone; the occurrence of the sexual act must depend, not on traditions, conventions, and rules of obligation, but on mutual accommodation and sympathy born of love and respect for personal integrity.

V

THE NATURE OF UNION IN 'ONE FLESH'

IT is customary and perhaps convenient to speak of husband and wife as 'partners' in marriage, and this is not an inaccurate description of their institutional relation with its contractual basis. But their ontological relation as a metaphysical coinherence in 'one flesh' cannot properly be designated a partnership. Sexual intercourse establishes and nourishes a new, organic, biune relation in which man and woman give themselves to one another entirely and without stipulation, yet so that while their independence is broken down, the individuality of each is enhanced and developed. In nothing do they live for themselves alone, but out of their separate lives a common life of distinctive character is built up by the sharing of everything they possess. Their sexual union both constitutes and symbolizes this unique, organic relation which in its essential nature is in no way comparable to a partnership, being founded upon love and not upon mutual agreement.

There is, however, one respect in which this self-surrender of husband and wife is not complete and unqualified; neither has the right to intrude into the other's relation with God, though each must inevitably be affected by the other's faith and prayer. Francis Thompson denounces the pseudo-romanticism of those lovers who would give themselves

wholly to one another in neglect, ignorance or defiance of God's claim upon man:

> *The sweetest wife on sweetest marriage-day—*
> *Their souls at grapple in mid-way,*
> *Sweet to her sweet may say:*

> *'I take you to my inmost heart, my true!'*
> *Ah, fool! but there is one heart you*
> *Shall never take him to!*

> .   .   .   .

> *Its keys are at the cincture hung of God;*
> *Its gates are trepidant to his nod;*
> *By him its floors are trod.*[1]

But marriage does not involve an apportionment between God and the beloved. While the secret 'one heart' must be preserved for its Maker in all its integrity, the whole 'one flesh' life must be consecrated to Him for His glory.

Husband and wife are also one with all 'flesh', not now as individuals, but as an organic biunity; their union, though secret and intimate to themselves, affords them no escape from human solidarity. Their change in status necessitates a mutual adjustment between themselves and the community of which they continue to form part—in fact, if they are Christians, there has to be a double adjustment, for they are members of the Church as well as of the secular community.

The emergence of these new relations accounts for the publicity accorded to marriage, and for the elaboration of religious and civil forms by which the community in question seeks to ascertain the *bona fides* of the parties, and signifies its approval and recognition of the union they contemplate. Such forms, however, do not establish the *henosis*; only the man and the woman themselves can do that. It is important that there should be no confusion between the initiation of the 'one

[1] *A Fallen Yew*, stanzas 17, 18 and 23 (*Works*, i, p. 183).

flesh' union by sexual intercourse and the solemnization of matrimony in church, or the civil registration of a marriage. The distinction between the ontological and the institutional aspects of the relation must be preserved. The Marriage Service is the place where the Church declares God's will in regard to sexual union and bestows her blessing upon those who, being faithful members of Christ's Body, come to affirm before God and the congregation their intention, by His grace, to 'live together after [His] ordinance in the holy estate of Matrimony' to which they believe they have been called. At the registry office those who desire to live as 'one flesh' but wish to dispense with a religious ceremony simply declare their intention before the competent authority and receive the community's permission for what they are about to do. But in neither case does the *henosis* actually come into existence until sexual intercourse has taken place.

The significance of the Marriage Service is weakened by the habitual omission of the Communion, and the restoration of its celebration is a much-needed reform. As the couple kneel at the altar and partake of the Sacrament of Unity they declare their solidarity in Christ with their fellow-members of His mystical Body, and the Church, in her administration of that Sacrament to them, recognizes their new status and their new relation to the whole company of the faithful.

The only difference—though it is a substantial and important one—between marriage and the responsible cohabitation of which Augustine writes in *de bono conjugali* is that in the case of the latter there is a refusal to acknowledge the fact of human solidarity, to admit the claim of the community upon the individual, and to accept in particular the paradox that in the most private and intimate of all relations society has a legitimate interest. Irresponsible cohabitation, prostitution, and other irregular relations, on the other hand, are in their different degrees defiant rejections of the community's rightful concern in a matter which affects it, and evasions of all that

'one flesh' implies. They mean the negation of the principles underlying sexual union, and the establishment of a false *henosis* which unites man and woman in rebellion against God and in alliance with the forces of social anarchy.

VI

INDISSOLUBILITY AND DIVORCE

DIVORCE is a subject of great complexity and difficulty concerning which Christians are not agreed. Here it is proposed simply to consider it with reference to the idea of 'one flesh', first briefly surveying the historical background.

Following what they understood to be Jesus' teaching, the Fathers of the Church generally held that marriage is indissoluble. They normally allowed, and sometimes required a husband to put away his wife for adultery or fornication, though towards an offending husband a more lenient attitude was often adopted, especially in the East, where the influence of secular law and common custom can be seen; there were, however, those like St. Basil[1] who felt the unfairness of this double standard. After divorce the 'guilty' party was forbidden to remarry, but there was no clear consensus of opinion in the case of the 'innocent' party; remarriage was usually prohibited, but some allowed it.[2] Separation or at least non-cohabitation,

---

[1] *Epist.* cxcix,21 *ad Amplioch.*

[2] Lactantius, *Inst.*, vi. 23; Epiphanius, *Haer.*, lix. 4; cf. the second Irish Synod, can. 26 (Haddan and Stubbs, *Councils*, II. ii, p. 337). Augustine held that such remarriage was only a venial error (*de fid. et. op.* 35 [xix]); Basil considered it pardonable, and that the woman who married the 'innocent' husband was not to be condemned (*Epist.* clxxxviii *ad Amplioch.* 9); in so far as its prohibition relates to the woman alone, *Conc. Elib.*, can. 8, may be interpreted as implying a right of remarriage to a deserted husband, and *Conc. Elib.*, can. 10, appears to concede a similar right to the man who legally divorces his wife. *Apost. Const.*, vi. 17, may be construed as permitting remarriage to a woman so long as she does not wed a cleric; Tertullian in his pre-Montanist days seems not to have disapproved, see *ad ux.* ii. 1; *Conc. Arelat.* I. can. 10, is ambiguous, however; see the discussion in Hefele, *Councils*, i, pp. 189–90, and in *Marriage in Church and State*, T. A. Lacey, rev. R. C. Mortimer (1947), pp. 101–2.

which amounted to the same thing, was sometimes required on ordination or elevation to the episcopate, and in such circumstances the wife was not permitted to remarry.

Only gradually did the Western Church succeed in enforcing acceptance of the principle of indissolubility, and in prohibiting remarriage after divorce, but this was finally accomplished by the eleventh century, and in the twelfth, through Gratian's *Decretum*, became the law and teaching in western Christendom. In the East, divorce with a right of remarriage was allowed on certain specified grounds.[1]

The Scholastic theology underlying this teaching, as set forth by St. Thomas, may be summarized thus. Since indissolubility belongs to the first intention of marriage as a sacrament of the Church, divorce is impossible for the Christian.[2] Although a man may put away his wife for fornication (except in seven specified cases, in most of which the offence is only formal or technical),[3] neither may remarry during the lifetime of the other.[4] A husband is not bound to put away an adulterous but repentant wife, and may be reconciled to her after separation, if she repents; but if she refuses to repent he must put her away and must on no account take her back.[5] The matter is not discussed from the woman's standpoint; St. Thomas considers it unfitting that she should put away her husband, since she is subject to his authority.[6]

According to the *Summa contra Gentiles* marriage is also indissoluble in natural law.[7] Its dissolution is an offence against equity, since a woman divorced when ageing stands at a disadvantage in securing another husband. It runs counter to the principle of order in human relation, because the female

---

[1] See Macmillan, *op. cit.*, pp. 89-92.

[2] *Summa Theol.*, III. Supp. lxvii 2 ad 3, suggests that dispensation from indissolubility in the case of Christian marriage might perhaps be effected by some supernatural means, just as a miracle suspends the natural course of things.

[3] *Summa Theol.*, III Supp. lxii 1 *resp.*

[4] *ibid.*, 5 *resp.*: '. . . nothing supervenient to marriage can dissolve it: wherefore adultery does not make a marriage cease to be valid."

[5] *ibid.*, 2 *resp.*; 6 *resp.*

[6] *Summa c. Gentiles*, iii. 123.   [7] *ibid.*

needs the male, not only for procreation but also for govern-ance—and this implies a life-long union. It denies, too, the principle of friendship which attains its highest expression in marriage, for the more intimate a relation, the more stable and enduring it will be. Finally, there is the fact that parental responsibility is never completely discharged—though in the *Summa Theologica* this is qualified: the good of the offspring only necessitates the indissolubility of marriage when parents have to provide for their children during the whole of life; consequently indissolubility belongs only to the secondary, and not to the primary precepts of the natural law. Hence it would seems, says St. Thomas (or his editor), that

. . . to put away one's wife is not contrary to the first in-tention of nature;

divorce and remarriage, therefore, were permissible by dispensation in the times before Christ.[1]

While the canonists of the Church rigidly maintained the doctrine of the indissolubility of marriage, it must not be overlooked that administration of the law often produced an effect opposite to that intended. Lacey says:

It cannot be denied that the medieval Canon law failed miserably as guardian of the holy estate[2]

and although Dr. Mortimer, in revising *Marriage in Church and State*, modifies some of the severer strictures of the original, he has still to admit that

. . . the intricacy of the law regarding impediments, the strictness with which it was applied, and the frequent occurrence of legal flaws in dispensations granted and received not always in good faith, made an immense number of marriages precarious.

[1] *Summa Theol.*, III Supp. lxvii 2 *resp.*
[2] *Marriage in Church and State* (orig. ed.), p. 159.

and cites the case of Henry VIII as one where there can clearly be seen

> . . . the complexity of the law, the influence of wealth and politics on its administration, and the general weakening of the sense of the sanctity and indissolubility of the marriage bond.[1]

To the teaching of the mediaeval Church the first formularies of Anglicanism bear accurate witness, declaring that the bond of matrimony cannot be dissolved except by death.[2] The Prayer Book makes no such express statement, though the bride and bridegroom promise to live together in prosperity or adversity until parted by death, and the priest, joining their hands, pronounces the dominical caution: 'Those whom God hath joined together, let no man put asunder.' Canon CVII of 1604 simply prohibits remarriage after 'divorce and separation *a thoro et mensa*'.

Among Anglican divines there has always been a difference of opinion. Some uphold the principle of indissolubility and forbid remarriage after divorce; others would allow remarriage to the 'innocent' party. Among the first, Andrewes asserted that adultery does not dissolve the marriage bond and that, in the event of divorce, both parties are inhibited from remarriage, which is not warranted by the word of God.[3] Hammond also will not permit remarriage, and would allow divorce for adultery only to the husband, and not to the wife, since the inconveniences of *confusio prolis* do not follow from the husband's adultery, and she, being in subjection to him, has no authority over him such as to enable her to put him away.[4] Comber states that

---

[1] Lacey-Mortimer, *op. cit.*, pp. 138–9.

[2] *Formularies of Faith put forth by authority during the reign of Henry VIII*, ed. C. Lloyd, p. 88; cf. pp. 91–2 (*The Institution of a Christian Man*); pp. 276–7 (*A Necessary Doctrine and Erudition for any Christian Man*).

[3] *Discourse against Second Marriage*, *Works* (Lib. of Angl.-Cath. Theol.), vi, pp. 106–7.

[4] *A Practical Catechism*, II, § vii, *Works* (Lib. of Angl.-Cath. Theol.), i, pp. 139–40. Wilkins, *History of Divorce and Remarriage*, p. 150, says that Hammond allows remarriage, but there is no express permission in the place mentioned.

... this bond of matrimony being rightly entered into can never be dissolved so long as both parties live together. In some cases there may be obtained a sentence of separation. ... But according to the rules of the church of England, the bond of matrimony remains in force after such separation. ... [1]

More recently the Tractarians and their successors have held similar views.

Many, however, have found the Church of England 'somewhat tender' in the matter of the prohibition of remarriage.[2] The classic expression of advanced Protestant opinion in England is the section *de adulteriis et divortiis* of the abortive *Reformatio Legum Ecclesiasticarum* compiled under Edward VI (who died before it could be enacted) and published in 1571. This code, which fortunately never attained legal force, proposed the abolition of divorce *a mensa et thoro* and made divorce absolute (with right of remarriage for the 'innocent' party) in the case of adultery, desertion, the unduly long absence of a partner, and certain kinds of irremediable incompatibility.[3] Here, no doubt, can be seen the influence of Continental Protestant immigrants like Martin Bucer and Peter Martyr, who advocated greater freedom of divorce and remarriage, and opposed dispensations and the doctrine of the sacramental character of marriage. But similar views are also to be found among the English Reformers,[4] and, with certain modifications, in the works of later writers of different schools. Thus Joseph Hall says:

I doubt not but I may, notwithstanding great authorities to the contrary, safely resolve that, in the case of divorce,

---

[1] *A Companion to the Temple*, The Office of Matrimony, IV. ii. § 5, *Works* (Oxford, 1841), iv, p. 100.

[2] See Hall, *Cases of Conscience*, Dec. IV, case iii, *Works* (Oxford 1837-9), vii, p. 474.

[3] *capita* 19, 5, 6, 9, and 11 (cf. 10).

[4] For example, Tyndale, on Matt. 5.31–2 in *Exposition of Matt. v. vi. and vii*, *Works* (Parker Society), ii, p. 55; cf. p. 51; Hooper, *A Declaration of the Ten Commandments*, ch. 10, *Works* (Parker Society), i, p. 384; cf. ii, p. xxiii, and *Original Letters* (Parker Society), p. 416.

it is lawful for the innocent person to marry. . . . I dare not ensnare those whom God would have free.[1]

Cosin held that adultery dissolved a marriage, though the arguments with which he supported the 'Act for John Manners, called Lord Roos, to marry again' do not carry great weight; there is no doubt that he misinterpreted the imposing mass of evidence which he collected from Patristic sources, though his own conviction is clear.[2] Thorndike contended that Christian marriage is indissoluble in point of right, but not in point of fact,[3] and approved divorce for adultery, allowing remarriage to the 'innocent' husband, but not to the wife put away.[4] He considered, however, that

> . . . the indissolubility of marriage, excepting our Lord's exception, is as firmly proved as the consent of the Church may prove anything in Christianity.[5]

To these instances from the sixteenth and seventeenth centuries it will suffice to add one or two of more recent date. Archbishop Frederick Temple held that a clergyman is not bound to say that the Church will not recognize the remarriage of an 'innocent' wife, and that one who married again could rightly claim admission to the Communion.[6] On another occasion he wrote:

> The Book of Common Prayer does not pronounce marriage indissoluble. It declares that whom God hath joined together no man may put asunder.

[1] *Cases of Conscience*, Dec. IV, case iii, *Works*, vii, p. 474; cf. p. 473.

[2] Some of his arguments are to be found in a paper, *Proving that Adultery works a dissolution of the Marriage*, *Works* (Lib. of Angl.-Cath. Theol.), iv, pp. 489–502. Gladstone described Cosin's treatment of the Scriptural evidence concerning the legality of remarriage as 'trumpery enough', *Letters on Church and Religion*, i, p. 134.

[3] *Of the Laws of the Church*, III, xiv, § 4, *Works* (Lib. Angl.-Cath. Theol.), iv, p. 309.

[4] *ibid.*, III, xiv, § 7 (*Works*, iv, pp. 312–13); cf. *The Reformation of the Church of England*, xxxvi, § 7 (*Works*, v, pp. 568–9).

[5] *ibid.*, III, xiv, § 26 (*Works*, iv, p. 323).

[6] *Memoirs*, ii, pp. 111–12.

Our Lord's exception in the case of adultery shows that a divorce in such a case is not man's doing but the Lord's.[1]

Bishop Walsham How reports a conversation in which Christopher Wordsworth, Bishop of Lincoln, professed himself

. . . quite convinced that the marriage of the innocent party after divorce must be allowed, however much to be deprecated.[2]

Bishop Mandell Creighton invokes the principle of equity and considers the remarriage of the 'innocent' party in a divorce 'a matter for our discretion', since the law of the Church had become unworkable when dispensations were abolished.[3] Even Bishop Gore writes that Jesus, in Matt. 5.32 and 19.9,

. . . appears . . . to make an exception, and the exception would seem to sanction, or, more strictly, not to prohibit, the remarriage of an innocent man who has put away his wife for adultery.[4]

These examples, which have been selected almost at random and could have been multiplied, will suffice to show the extent of both strict and liberal opinion within Anglicanism. The Resolutions of the Lambeth Conferences over the last seventy years reveal a tendency towards the stricter view. In 1908 a Resolution of 1888 was affirmed which recognized the difference of opinion in the Church and recommended that the Sacraments and other privileges of the Church should not be refused to an 'innocent' party who had remarried after divorce.[5] In 1920 the Conference admitted

. . . the right of a national or regional Church within our Communion to deal with cases which fall within the exception mentioned in the record of our Lord's words in St.

[1] *Memoirs*, ii, pp. 293–4. [2] *Life*, p. 474. [3] *Life and Letters*, ii, pp. 68–9.
[4] *The Sermon on the Mount*, p. 71; cf. pp. 215ff. [5] Resolution 39 C.

Matthew's Gospel, under provisions which such Church may lay down.[1]

In 1930, however, while passing no judgement on the practice of regional or national Churches, the Conference recommended

. . . that the marriage of one, whose former partner is still living, should not be celebrated according to the rites of the Church,[2]

while in 1948 it declared that such a marriage

. . . may not be celebrated according to the rites of the Church, unless it has been established that there exists no marriage bond recognized by the Church.[3]

But, in spite of these disciplinary rulings, it is clear that the difference of opinion remains.

Our survey shows that the official teaching of the Western Church until the Reformation, and of the Anglican Church thereafter, has always been that marriage is indissoluble except by death, that divorce is permissible for adultery, and that remarriage after divorce is to be forbidden. It shows also that some of the early Fathers and many Anglican divines tended to favour the allowance of remarriage after divorce to the 'innocent' party, and that in mediaeval times the granting of dispensations produced a state of affairs in which the dissolution of numerous marriages constituted a practical denial of the canon law theory and the Church's theology. Two questions now concern us: What does 'indissoluble' really mean? and, What is the basis of the Church's official teaching?

'Indissoluble', as Dr. Kirk has observed, may mean *'ought not* to be dissolved', or *'cannot* be dissolved'.[4] Christians are

---

[1] Resolution 67.

[2] Resolution 11 (*a*); admission of the 'innocent' party to Holy Communion after remarriage is to be referred to the Bishop (11 [*b*]).

[3] Resolution 94; Resolution 96 restates Resolution 11 (*b*) of 1930 in more definite terms.

[4] *Marriage and Divorce*, p. 13.

universally agreed that marriage ought not to be dissolved, but if this is all the Church means by 'indissoluble', the problem of divorce and remarriage would not have caused such difficulty and division of opinion. By many, however, the union of husband and wife is regarded as incapable of dissolution, and the divorce permitted by the Church as in fact only a separation —it is *a mensa et thoro*, not *a vinculo*.

But when we enquire what actually constitutes the indissoluble element in marriage, we immediately encounter difficulty. Does it lie in the mutual contract, or in something effected thereby? Bride and bridegroom certainly bind themselves publicly by a solemn undertaking to remain faithful to one another until death, no matter what befalls them, but this does not and cannot, of itself, bring into existence a relation which is essentially permanent and indissoluble. The "vow and covenant" between them has no ontological consequences, but simply gives expression to a serious and considered intention, and embodies the terms upon which they propose to contract marriage. The plighting and the giving of their troth lays upon them both a moral obligation of the utmost weight, but that is all.

Does the element of indissolubility, then, lie in something effected by the sexual intercourse which consummates the marriage union? The sexual act certainly establishes the 'one flesh' *henosis*, and brings about an ontologcial change both in the man and the woman themselves and in their relation. Neither can ever be again as they were before they came together; each does something to the other that is ineffaceable. But while intercourse has indelible personal consequences, and initiates a new and unique relation, it does not effect an indissoluble union. There are, for instance, certain false states of 'one flesh' which are by their nature ephemeral, such as that resulting from fornication. It has already been shown that a union in 'one flesh' is valid or false according to the character of the sexual act by which it was established, and that the latter

is determined by the intention of the parties, and by the context of their intercourse. What is true of the initiation of the relation must also hold good in regard to its continuance. Upon love alone the validity of intercourse and the permanence and exclusiveness of marriage depend, and love means nothing if not freely-willed, unqualified fidelity. The sexual act in which love finds its sacramental expression does not, as it were, *ex opere operato*, effect an indissoluble union; it is, between husband and wife, simply a profound and significant affirmation of their attitude towards their relation, and in particular, of their intention to remain absolutely faithful to the letter and the spirit of their mutual "vow and covenant".

It follows that the conditions which determine the inward validity of a 'one flesh' union may cease to exist—in other words, that love may fail. Such a possibility is repugnant to pseudo-romantic idealism, but it must not, on that account be ignored. Love depends for its existence upon a true *I-Thou* relation, and between its recurrent personal encounters in the world of *Thou*, is sustained by fidelity; when this moral element of fidelity fails, it means the failure of love. The internal disintegration of the 'one flesh' union is then inevitable; its progress may be arrested by the stabilization of a 'defective' *henosis*, or it may end in dissolution—but not necessarily in separation (divorce), for the appearance of marriage may still be kept up.

The bearing of the failure of love upon the problem of divorce and remarriage deserves some further consideration at this point. Love alone gives meaning and inward validity to marriage, and guarantees its integrity; without it there can be no union of husband and wife in 'one flesh', but only a legalized cohabitation possessing no ontological significance. This view, of course, finds no place in the traditional, predominantly institutional conception of marriage, but it is clear that the latter cannot satisfactorily be described otherwise than in terms of personal relation; that is to say, it is rooted and

grounded in a distinctive *I-Thou* experience—sexual love. This love, as Buber observes, 'cannot persist in direct relation', and 'endures . . . in interchange of actual and potential being';[1] it would vanish during the abeyance of the recurrent relational experience, were it not for the moral element of fidelity to the *Thou* who for the time being is *She*, either present and observed or absent and recollected. Moreover, there is essentially a hopeful note in this fidelity; where the love is mutual and complete it is always potentially in existence; both lover and beloved pass the interval in which each belongs to the other's world of *It* in assured and joyful expectation of the renewal of their meeting in the world of *Thou*.

This moral element of fidelity is given expression in the 'vow and covenant' which bride and bridegroom exchange at the Marriage Service. Their mutual promise is something more than a mere contractual engagement; it is unique among human undertakings in that its inner significance and indeed its intrinsic worth, no less than the fulfilment of its terms, depend upon the distinctive personal relation of sexual love. Hence marriage is always precarious; fidelity alone, as the expression of a sense of obligation or duty, may preserve it as an institution, but only fidelity as an element in love can guarantee its ontological validity. When love fails beyond all hope of revival, a marriage is dead, no matter how desperately husband or wife may cling to the empty, lifeless shell of their relation. Those who become 'one flesh', therefore, need to be constantly watchful and sensitive to one another; to take love for granted means that one who was *Thou* is henceforth only *She*.

Since nothing but the failure of love can cause the dissolution of a 'one flesh' union it ought, strictly speaking, to constitute the sole and sufficient ground of divorce. Here, however, serious difficulties are encountered. The community is concerned with the disruption of marriage no less than with its establishment, for social stability and morality are

1 See above, p. 12.

[80]

endangered, and divorce ought not to be granted without sufficient cause and adequate investigation. But it is always impossible to determine when and to what extent a personal relation has broken down, for no reliable and convincing evidence can be secured. That is why both Church and secular community have been prepared to allow divorce for adultery; the very fact of its occurrence constitutes acceptable evidence that the marriage has failed, and there is usually good reason for considering its rehabilitation improbable. It is arguable that divorce should be permitted for other causes than adultery, but the cessation of love could never be allowed as one of them; it would be too difficult to verify, and against public policy as too open to abuse. That, however, ought not to prevent its being recognized as the fundamental cause of the disintegration of the 'one flesh' union and therefore, in theory, the only admissible ground for divorce. Here again we observe the paradoxical situation which arises inevitably from the rightful concern of the community in an essentially personal and private matter. To this can ultimately be traced most of the difficulties attendant upon marriage breakdown. The regulation of such a personal relation in the interests of the common good is bound to produce tensions which cannot easily be resolved, and in particular, to result in all too little account being taken of the love from which marriage derives its inner meaning.

The failure of love and the consequent disintegration of a 'one flesh' union are clearly the fruit of sin—and not infrequently, the sin of entering marriage 'unadvisedly, lightly, or wantonly'. In some few cases the terms 'innocent party' and 'guilty party' are permissible, but in most cases the responsibility must be shared, though not always equally. When a marriage relation breaks down it does not necessarily mean that all hope of its restoration is past; repentance and forgiveness may lead to reunion and the establishment of a true *henosis* in conformity with the will of God as an act of reparation and

satisfaction. And even if no restoration is possible, the sinfulness of the failure requires penitence on the part of husband and wife alike—but being penitent for the sin of the past, and legally free by divorce, is either to be allowed to remarry?

This question may be expressed differently: When a personal relation so distinctive as sexual love breaks down, is another such relation subsequently possible and permissible? There can be no doubt that a second love-relation is possible after a first has come to an end, and there can be no doubt also that if it is genuine it will seek to achieve its consummation in a second 'one flesh' union. This seems to violate no relational principle. When the love which unites husband and wife fails, their marriage loses all ontological significance, and therefore all essential justification for its continuance; it is strictly irrelevant to the relational situation that the interests of the community or social expediency may make it necessary to maintain the pretence that all is well. Breakdown, and even divorce, however, need not be final; they need not mean permanent separation. Penitence, reconciliation, and a new experience of love can lead to the emergence of a new 'one flesh' union between those who were once husband and wife and who, through the sin and pain of relational failure, have been brought by the Spirit to a new mind and a desire to atone for the past. But when this happens, it does not mean that the former relation has been resuscitated; that is impossible, for the love which was once between them has been destroyed and can never be revived. Rather, a new love has been born out of penitence and forgiveness; they have entered into a new relation, entirely distinct from the old, yet conditioned for ever by a purged recollection of the failure which has been redeemed.

For the reconciliation of those whose marriages have broken down it is clear that the Church has a primary responsibility. This is not to say that individuals, and organizations such as the Marriage Guidance Councils, may not also be the

instruments through which God wills to bring together again those whose love for each other has died. But the Church cannot escape its obligations, or delegate them to others. Often it is only through a sympathetic and informed pastoral ministry that a new relation, doubly grounded in penitence for the past and in hope for the future, can be satisfactorily realized; indeed, it is difficult to see how there can be real repentance apart from the Church (whether or not use is made of the sacrament of Penance). It is of great importance, therefore, that the Church should make available a skilled ministry of this kind, and that it should do all in its power to remove those common misconceptions concerning its attitude towards sexual relation, which might discourage resort to such a ministry of reconciliation.

But repentance and pardon may not, and often do not lead to a rebirth of love, and so to a new 'one flesh' union in which reparation is made for the sin of the past. Usually there is no prospect of the divorced husband and wife entering again into relation—there may, indeed, be good reason why they should avoid doing so. May one or both then contract a new marriage? Consider the position in terms of personal relation: a marriage which has broken down and disintegrated is no longer a union in 'one flesh', for the love from which alone it derived validity and meaning is dead; the marriage is an empty shell, wholly devoid of inner significance, long before divorce reveals the true state of affairs. All this, however, does not in itself justify remarriage; for this, there must be penitence and forgiveness for the sin which caused the breakdown. The failure of love can destroy the *henosis*, and civil divorce may annul the marriage, but only repentance can sever the bond of guilt for their failure which still unites husband and wife to one another. Without that repentance and all that it must cost, they are tied together and cannot escape—or to express it differently, the first, broken marriage hangs round their necks like the dead albatross round the neck of the Ancient Mariner,

and only penitence can lose the cord. When relational failure (and divorce) occur, a union does not simply go out of existence: in some sense it continues as a bad, dead thing, and can only be terminated by the penitence through which the sin of husband and wife is redeemed. Nor, when the penitence is not on both sides, is the repentant one bound to the unrepentant; it is for each individually to sever the connexion with the dead but persistent marriage, the sinful and tragic past.

For the impenitent, then, it is clear that there ought to be no permission to remarry, but the case of the repentant is different; there it seems that with proper safeguards a second union might be allowed. Such a concession, it is recognized, would involve pastoral and disciplinary considerations which fall outside the scope of this essay, and would mean a departure from the general teaching of the Church in the West which would certainly encounter no little opposition. Some of the grounds upon which it would be contested, such as the indissolubility of marriage, have already been discussed, but two others now require examination.

While allowing that the 'vow and covenant' exchanged at the Marriage Service cannot effect an ontologically indissoluble relation, there are many who would maintain that it imposes upon husband and wife an obligation from which no circumstance can relieve them. In this view, not even the death of love, the breakdown of the marriage, and divorce can annul the troth once plighted and given; the promise is unconditionally binding, so that even in the event of adultery or desertion the faithful partner must keep to the unfaithful until released by the death of the latter. If this interpretation of the 'vow and covenant' is correct, remarriage during the lifetime of a divorced partner is clearly wrong, but it is open to serious doubt whether such an interpretation is tenable. It seems to be based upon a misunderstanding of the promise itself. The terms of the mutual stipulation show plainly that bride and bridegroom do not exchange an unqualified promise. John pledges

fidelity, not to Mary, but to Mary-married; Mary pledges fidelity, not to John, but to John-married. That is to say, both imply that their 'vow and covenant' is to be operative, not absolutely, but in a certain context; 'living faithfully together', they are to perform and keep it. Fidelity is promised to the faithful. The one's infidelity does not automatically release the other from the undertaking given at the Marriage Service, but it necessitates a decision as to whether, under the circumstances, that undertaking is any longer to be considered binding. The pledge of faithfulness is not simply a personal pledge made to someone; it is a personal pledge made with reference to a particular personal relation, and for the purpose of that relation. When love fails and a marriage breaks down beyond all hope of restoration, it is difficult to see what real meaning attaches any longer to the 'vow and covenant'.

Even if it were conceded, however, that the promises exchanged by bride and bridegroom are only conditionally binding,[1] the strongest objection to divorce *a vinculo* with permission to remarry would yet remain, for the doctrine and law of the Church are based primarily upon the teaching of Jesus as recorded in Mark 10.2–12, Matt. 5.32 and 19.3–12, and Luke 16.18—with which may be considered St. Paul's teaching in I Cor. 7.10-11 and 12-15. It is well-known that the two Matthaean passages are distinguished from the other Synoptic material by the addition of the words [*ei*] *mē epi porneia* ('except for fornication') or *parektos logou porneias* ('saving for the cause of fornication'), and that scholars are generally agreed, on text-critical grounds, in regarding these clauses as additions to our Lord's teaching by way of interpretation. Since Matthew's handling of his material is suspect, it will be better to examine first the Marcan account, comparing it where necessary with the Matthaean.

---

[1] 'For better, for worse' would not seem to apply to breakdown and divorce, as some think, though it may imply a deterioration within marriage. Comber, *op. cit.* (*Works*, iv, p. 96), says it means 'howsoever their minds be qualified, or whatever their manners shall be'.

According to Mark, Jesus was asked: 'Is it lawful for a man to put away his wife?'—a strange question from Jews,[1] who had no doubt as to the legality of divorce, though at that time most of them looked upon it with repugnance. It may be that the enquiry arose out of some previous and unrecorded teaching, or that there were some among the Lord's followers who were genuinely doubtful whether divorce was really accordant with the will of God; 'tempting him', however, may indicate that the object was to extract from Jesus an unorthodox pronouncement upon the Mosaic Law. Matthew's addition, 'for every cause', gives point to the question by relating it to a discussion then beginning to arise concerning the interpretation of the Law in Deut. 24.1–4. It is often stated that the First Evangelist makes Jesus agree with Shammai against Hillel, but Abrahams says,

> It is uncertain whether this particular difference of opinion on divorce[2] goes back to Hillel and Shammai themselves, and thus to the very beginning of the Christian era.[3]

There is every probability, however, that the latter controversy grew out of a general debate on the subject of 'putting away', in connexion with which Jesus' opinion would be sought. The exact form of the question put to Him is made irrelevant by his answer: Moses allowed divorce because of man's *sklēro-kardia*, but the purpose of God in creating man and woman is that they shall become 'one flesh' in marriage. He does not assert that their union is ontologically indissoluble, but he utters the emphatic prohibition:

> What therefore God hath joined together, let not man put asunder.

[1] The reference to 'Pharisees' is omitted by Codex Bezae, certain Old Latin MSS., Codex Syr. Sinaiticus, and the Sahidic Egyptian text. It has been brought into Mark from Matthew, who added it to the original when incorporating it into his Gospel: see C. H. Turner in *A New Commentary, ad loc.*

[2] i.e., as to the meaning of '. . . if she find no favour in his eyes, because he hath found some unseemly thing in her. . . .'

[3] *Studies in Pharisaism and the Gospels*, Series I, p. 71.

This might be paraphrased: When a man and a woman, fulfilling the purpose of God, have become 'one flesh' through sexual intercourse, neither a third party nor a man-made law must be allowed to disrupt their union. That is to say, Jesus asserts in the strongest possible terms the moral obligation to lifelong fidelity which the Divine will imposes upon husband and wife; He implies that the work of God in calling them together and making them 'one flesh' cannot be undone without grave sin. But He knows that its undoing is possible, for He knows what is in man. This, however, does not prevent Him from declaring very clearly what marriage is in its essence; hence He refuses to enter the contemporary discussion, and goes behind it, as He goes behind the Mosaic Law, in order to show that 'from the beginning' God had purposed for man and woman the mysterious destiny of union in 'one flesh'. In effect, Jesus turns the subject under consideration from divorce to the nature of marriage, and His teaching, therefore, is not properly comparable to that of the Rabbis; Hillel and Shammai, as G. F. Moore observes,

. . . were jurisconsults called upon to pronounce authoritatively what the law was; while Jesus, having no such authority or responsibility, undertook to say what, on ideal principles, the law ought to be, Moses to the contrary notwithstanding.[1]

So far there is no essential conflict between the Marcan and the Matthaean accounts. We now turn to Jesus' teaching on adultery and remarriage, which was given to the disciples according to Mark, privately 'in the house'. It is reproduced by Matthew with the significant exception already mentioned, and appears also in a parallel Q passage of which Matthew and Luke preserve different versions. Matthew, omitting any reference to the private nature of the teaching, makes it part of the account just considered (19.1–8), while the Q passages

[1] *Judaism*, ii, p. 125.

appear in two contexts—the Matthaean in the Sermon on the Mount, the Lucan among some sayings spoken against Pharisees. Short though these four pronouncements are, they display a remarkable lack of consistency; the six following statements can be distinguished:

1. Every man who puts away his wife and remarries commits adultery (Luke 16.18 [Q]).
2. Every man who puts away his wife and remarries commits adultery against her (Mark 10.11).
3. Every man who puts away his wife (except for *porneia*) and remarries commits adultery (Matt. 19.9*a*).
4. Every man who puts away his wife (except for *porneia*) makes her an adulteress (Matt. 5.32*a*).
5. Every man who marries a woman put away commits adultery (Matt. 19.9*b*; Luke 16.18*b* [Q]; Matt. 5.32*b* [Q])—though whether this holds good if she is put away for *porneia* is not clear.
6. A woman who puts away her husband and remarries commits adultery (Mark 10.12).

Several difficulties arise out of these statements. They are not apparent when 'put away' is taken as equivalent to divorce in the modern sense, and 'adultery' is given its present day. meaning, but it must be remembered that Jesus' teaching was delivered to Jews against the background of Jewish law and custom. Now it is clear that

In Jewish law adultery was the intercourse of a married woman with *any* man other than her husband. . . . A man was not regarded as guilty of adultery unless he had intercourse with a *married* woman other than his wife.[1]

In no sense recognized by the law or intelligible to those who lived under it, therefore, could remarriage after divorce make

[1] Abrahams, *op. cit.*, p. 73; cf. his article on *Adultery (Jewish)* in *Encyclopaedia of Religion and Ethics*, i, p. 130*a*.

a man an adulterer; having put away his wife, he was legally free to contract another union. He could only commit adultery if he then had intercourse with a married woman, or with a betrothed girl—though the latter might become his wife. Nor could a man who married a divorced woman properly be said to commit adultery, since the 'bill of divorcement' declared her free to remarry.[1] Finally, the question of a woman putting away her husband never arose:

> . . . the divorce was always, from first to last, in Jewish law the husband's act.[2]

She could, however, ask an adulterous husband for a divorce, and he could release her if he chose; or in certain circumstances she could even claim one. It does not seem that the statement in Mark 10.12 refers to this; it may be an allusion to the practice whereby, after the Roman fashion, the wife could repudiate her marriage by serving upon her husband a 'bill of divorcement'—an innovation condemned by Josephus[3]—but far more probably it is a Marcan interpolation or amendment relating to the situation under Roman law. There is general agreement that 'except for *porneia*' in Matt. 19.9 is a qualification by the Evangelist, and probably rests upon Church tradition; it is usually interpreted as an attempt to relate Jesus' teaching to the Hillel-Shammai controversy, and shows Him favourable to the stricter Rabbi. By ignoring Mark 10.10 and joining this passage to the previous one (19.1–8), Matthew introduces a contradiction into Jesus' discourse, though this disappears with the omission of the excepting clause. The qualifying phrase itself has been variously explained. It is commonly held that it was either 'legislative' (the primitive Church having found it necessary to make such an exception in applying the principles laid down by our Lord), or explanatory (the Evangelist believing that Jesus' teaching implied, as

---

[1] Abrahams, *Studies in Pharisaism . . .* Series I, p. 70.
[2] *ibid.*, p. 72.   [3] *Ant.*, XV. vii. 11; XVIII. v. 5.

the disciples would understand, that adultery virtually dissolved a marriage, entitling the husband to divorce his wife and contract another union). Matt. 5.32 is very perplexing; it seems impossible to make sense of the words 'maketh her an adulteress'. They cannot mean that to divorce a wife on grounds other than adultery is to treat her as though she were an adulteress, for divorce was not in itself disgraceful, and might occur for reasons which implied no moral stigma.[1] Nor can they mean that to put away a wife who is not an adulteress amounts to making her one, since she is forced to marry again (which is tantamount to adultery?) in order to avoid destitution.[2] First, her remarriage would not be regarded under Judaism as adultery, for the divorce makes her a free agent; second, if she were put away on grounds other than *porneia* she would be entitled to the provision usually settled upon her at marriage against such an eventuality, and would not, therefore, be wholly destitute.[3]

As they stand, these four sayings of Jesus (Mark 10.11–12; Matt. 5.32 and 19.9; Luke 16.18) would have been quite unintelligible to a Jewish audience, and it is difficult now to determine what they mean in their original, non-modern sense. There can be no doubt that our Lord said more about divorce and remarriage than the Synoptists record, and the suspicion cannot be avoided that their brief, almost 'journalistic' reports omit certain essential steps and explanations in His argument; a Johannine discourse on marriage and divorce might well have revealed why He used 'adultery' in a sense which must have perplexed many of His hearers. As it is, we can only take care not to interpret Jesus' words anachronistically or in terms of contemporary non-Jewish usage, bearing in mind, however, that in the Marcan and Lucan versions they may have undergone some redaction with reference to a Gentile situation.

Whatever Jesus meant by 'adultery', the sayings clearly

[1] Abrahams, *op. cit.*, p. 73.
[2] As is suggested, for instance, in Lacey-Mortimer, *op. cit.*, p. 20.
[3] See Moore, *op. cit.*, ii, p. 123.

show that He regarded putting away and remarriage as somehow morally reprehensible, and was concerned above all to
declare the absolute will of God for man and woman. Two
explanations of His words are possible. They may be a condemnation of that liberal interpretation of the Law associated
with Hillel, according to which divorce was permissible even
for trivial reasons, including the desire to marry a fairer
woman.[1] Our Lord condemns as adulterous and immoral,
therefore, every high-handed and irresponsible act of putting
away, and especially, perhaps, divorce as a step towards
marrying another and more attractive woman; this is certainly
suggested by the close connexion between 'shall put away'/
'putteth away' and '[shall] marry another' (Mark 10.11; Matt.
19.9*a*; Luke 16.18*a*). The insertion of the Matthaean clause
'except for *porneia*' is then easily understood; the Evangelist
wished to make it clear that Jesus was not referring to the
'responsible' act of putting away an adulterous wife in obedience to the courts or out of deference to public opinion. So
indefensible, however, is putting away for a trivial cause that
our Lord will not recognize it as divorce; he who marries a
woman so put away really enters into relations with one who
is still a wife, and therefore commits adultery (Matt. 19.9*b*;
Luke 16.18*b*).

On the other hand, Jesus may have employed 'adultery'
as a forceful and challenging synonym for unfaithfulness. In
contemporary Jewish legal usage it meant, as we have seen,
grave and even criminal infidelity on the part of a married
woman. In Jesus' eyes, however, there could be no essential
difference between this and any other kind of marital unfaithfulness; every act of infidelity merited the same severe censure,
and could, therefore, be justly termed 'adultery'. No other
word could so clearly expose the true character of the sin which
severed the union of man and woman in 'one flesh'. To use
'adultery' in this way, however, would be to give it a new

---

[1] R. Akiba; see *Gittin*, ix. 10.

meaning, and it is possible that Jesus intended to do so. In Jewish eyes, the unfaithfulness of an adulteress was an offence committed against her husband, but Jesus' teaching implies that it was also an offence committed against God and against the marriage itself, as the expression of the Divine will and calling. It was a sin and a wrong of such a kind as to issue inevitably in the dissolution of a 'one flesh' union. Judaism, legislating from an androcentric standpoint, concerned itself less with the adulterer than with the wronged husband, but in our Lord's view the former could not but be fully implicated in the sin committed by his partner in adultery.

On this interpretation, the absence of any qualifying clause in the Marcan and Lucan versions of the sayings may be due to the writers' conviction that Jesus had refused to admit the validity of the Rabbinic legal distinctions as to putting away, and had insisted on applying new principles—the principles of 'one flesh'—to divorce and remarriage. Clearly, on those principles, the man who puts away his wife for some cause other than adultery and then contracts another union can be held guilty of grave infidelity towards the marriage (Luke 16.18a) and towards the wife divorced (Mark 10.11); ignorantly or deliberately he has transgressed a Divine ordinance. The same goes for the woman who requires an adulterous husband to divorce her, or who takes advantage of alien customs or laws to repudiate her marriage (Mark 10.12); she cannot avoid acting unfaithfully even if, as in the first case, she can justify her action. But what of proved adultery, where the law required divorce and the husband was not allowed to condone his wife's infidelity, nor to take her back? Here Jesus seems to imply that what is legally permissible or necessary is nevertheless, in the light of absolute standards, morally questionable; in divorcing his wife the husband shows himself as unfaithful to the marriage as the wife in her adultery, and if he remarries he confirms, as it were, his unfaithfulness. Matthew's [*ei*] *mē epi porneia* or *parektos logou porneias* is then to be explained

as a qualification designed to meet this admittedly awkward and difficult case (Matt. 19.9*a* and 5.32*a*); where there existed no legal obligation to put away a wife, the application of Jesus' principle was easier. But the statement that the man who marries a divorced woman is guilty of 'adultery' (grave infidelity) (Matt. 19.9*b* and 5.32*b*; Luke 16.18*b*) is still in some respects perplexing. Does it mean that by uniting with her he shares her own unfaithfulness?—though if she were put away for some cause that did not imply any moral stigma, it is hard to see where her infidelity could lie, unless it was her duty to remain free in case her husband, as sometimes happened, desired to receive her back and remarry her.

Neither interpretation of these difficult sayings is entirely satisfactory, and no alternative explanation seems possible unless the contemporary reference of Jesus' words is ignored and 'adultery' is given a modern, and therefore anachronistic connotation. Admittedly it is not easy to decide precisely what meaning He Himself gives to this term, but there can be no doubt that He condemns divorce-and-remarriage in certain circumstances as morally reprehensible—indeed, it is possible to interpret the sayings as unqualified denunciations of remarriage, and as such they have often been understood. Although our Lord did not expressly pronounce marriage indissoluble in the impossibilist sense, He may, on this latter view, have prohibited remarriage after divorce on disciplinary grounds. If so, there is clearly an insoluble tension between the Scriptural idea of marriage and the 'one flesh' union conceived in terms of a distinctive personal relation ontologically based upon love. On the other hand, Jesus' teaching may legitimately be interpreted as laying upon husband and wife a moral obligation to preserve absolute fidelity to one another,[1] while not disallowing divorce and remarriage where special circumstances can be held to justify them. That is to say, He condemns putting away for arbitrary or trivial reasons, especially with a

---

[1] See also Matt. 5.27–8.

view to a second union, but by implication does not prohibit the husband from seeking or consenting to dissolution of a marriage for any grave cause, such as the Law allowed. In spite of the textual evidence against its authenticity, the Matthaean qualification seems to represent an intelligible attempt to clarify an otherwise obscure passage.

The two Pauline passages need not detain us long. In I Cor. 7.10–11 the Apostle transmits a command from the Lord to this effect: A wife ought not to separate (*chōristhēnai*) from her husband—though if she does, she ought to remain unmarried, or else be reconciled to him—and a husband ought not to put away (*aphienai*) his wife. There is no difficulty here. According to the Law, upon which this injunction is based, though it is addressed to Gentile converts, a woman had no power of divorce; hence mere separation does not terminate the marriage, and she is not free to remarry. The emphasis, however, is still upon the need for fidelity: the wife ought not to desert her husband, and the husband ought not to divorce his wife. In the case of a mixed marriage (I Cor. 7.12–15) St. Paul counsels the pagan and Christian partners to continue living together so long as the former desires it; if, however, the unbeliever departs (*chōrizetai*), let him go—'the brother or the sister is not under bondage (*ou dedoulōtai*) in such cases'. This 'Pauline privilege', as it is often called, has been held to authorize the remarriage of a convert after desertion by the pagan partner, but its meaning is somewhat obscure. Commentators have found it difficult to agree upon the interpretation of *dedoulōmai* ('enslaved' or 'reduced to a state of bondage'). It may imply that the believer is not 'bound' to the marriage, and is therefore free to contract another union (as the Church has always taught), or it may simply mean that there is no obligation to continue cohabitation—the believer may consent to separation if the other desires it. The first explanation seems on the whole the more satisfactory.

The Jewish character of the injunction in the first passage

(which, as St. Paul makes clear, is not his, but the Lord's), suggests that the sayings about divorce and remarriage recorded by the Synoptists may have been rigorized in the course of transmission, and that Jesus' teaching, at least in certain respects, anticipated that of Shammai. This would tend to explain some of the obscurities already noticed, and to account for the Matthaean qualification as an attempt to correct the drastic editing of Mark and Q.

At present it seems impossible to reach any conclusion on divorce and remarriage which does justice alike to the special personal problems connected with marriage breakdown, to Scriptural teaching as traditionally interpreted by the Church, and to the relational principles discussed in the foregoing pages. These last in particular may necessitate a radical reconsideration of the whole subject sooner or later, but it is not the purpose of this study to embark upon any such undertaking, nor to attempt a reconciliation of the conflict of opinion which has existed in Anglicanism since the Reformation. Rather, it has been simply to indicate at this point the extent of that conflict and the real magnitude of the problem; and, as a contribution towards a solution, to suggest:

1. That it is misleading and inaccurate to continue to speak of marriage as a union incapable of dissolution;

2. That the Scriptural accounts of our Lord's teaching need further examination, due regard being paid to its contemporary reference, and consequently, to the possibility of alternative interpretations;

3. That divorce and remarriage must be considered seriously in terms of personal relation, recognizing that love is the ontological basis of the 'one flesh' union and is sustained by the moral element of fidelity, and that when love fails, no marriage any longer possesses inner validity or significance;

4. That while the failure of love destroys the *henosis*, it does not automatically dissolve every bond between husband and wife; only repentance can set free those who were married,

and whose relation has broken down beyond any possibility of restoration. Instead, therefore, of allowing remarriage after divorce to the 'innocent' party, as many have wished, and still wish the Church to do, it seems that it ought rather to be permitted to the repentant, and to them only.

VII

'ONE FLESH' AND THE RESURRECTION OF THE DEAD

WHEN the Sadducees sought to ridicule the idea of resurrection by suggesting that the custom of the levirate could produce a ludicrous problem of polyandry in the world to come, Jesus declared:

> . . . when they shall rise from the dead, they neither marry, nor are given in marriage; but are as angels in heaven.[1]

That is to say, the union of husband and wife in 'one flesh' belongs to the order of things that is passing away, and endures only until they are parted by death. It is so deeply and firmly rooted in man's physical nature that nothing comparable can exist in the world of spirit. Moreover, it is a personal relation which can only continue in being through the occurrence of successive meetings in the world of *Thou*, and is sustained during the intervals between each relational experience and the next by hope grounded in fidelity. This does not mean that love will not survive the dissolution of the body, and that there will be no social life or mutual recognition in the world to come. The Christian believes that relations such as love (which is the essential element in marriage) will endure, and will even be intensified in the Resurrection—yet in a manner

[1] Mark 12.25; cf. Matt 22.30 and Luke 20.34-5.

appropriate to those who will then be 'equal unto the angels'. We can be certain that nothing in personal relation which has meant much to us this side of the grave will be lost to us beyond it, although a transformation is inevitable.

But there our certainty must necessarily stop. We know, and can conceive, nothing of the conditions of the next life, save that it will be spiritual. We may, if we wish, speculate with St. Thomas Aquinas upon the possibility that there is a profound difference between the male and the female soul, just as there is between the male and the female body, and that this distinction will necessitate some sexual differentiation in the spiritual body.[1] Of this there can be no satisfactory proof, but if it were so, the absence of any need for procreation[2] would not, according to our understanding of the personal value of sex, preclude sexual experience in heaven—indeed, dissociated from generation, 'intercourse' (for we can only call it that) might there prove to be a relational factor of unsuspected significance.

It is salutary that those who become 'one flesh' should understand the transience, the 'fleshly' nature of the *henosis*. To-day a widespread pseudo-romanticism fosters the extravagant illusion that in sexual love there inheres some quality which exempts it from temporal limitation and invests it with immortality. In so doing, it refuses to recognize God's redemptive purpose in Christ whereby there is set before the creation the hope of deliverance from the bondage of corruption into the glorious liberty of the children of God.[3] It also denies the meaning of resurrection, which is always a mighty act of God done beyond human extremity; nothing belonging to present vanity, not even love, is immune from mortality in its own right. This, however, will not offend the Christian. He will

---

[1] *Summa Theol.*, III. Supp. lxxx 3.

[2] *ibid.*, 4 *sed contra; Compendium Theologiae*, c. 156; generation would be void of purpose in Heaven, since the race will be complete and deathless—cf. Luke 20.36: '. . . neither can they die any more'.

[3] Rom. 8.19ff.; cf. the 'mystery' of God's purpose declared in the Epistle to the Ephesians.

accept the vanity of the 'one flesh' because he knows that among the things which are passing away are human relations, and that, far from being scandalous, the *matiotēs* to which the creation has been subjected is for its own sake.[1] Not only does he share this present hope of eschatological deliverance, however; he knows too that in Christ the 'one flesh' is no longer devoid of ultimate meaning. It is redeemed, and becomes a place of training in sanctity. Thus marriage does not mean a way of escape from all that is transient into a world of illusion where mortality and God lose their significance and 'love' is the final reality; it means, rather, acceptance of the 'one flesh' in all its vanity as a relation in which God's will is nevertheless uniquely made known, and into which men and women are called by Him to fulfil it.

VIII

THE ENDS OF MARRIAGE AND OF UNION IN 'ONE FLESH'

SCRIPTURE itself says very little about the purpose of marriage. The earlier creation narrative suggests that it is unitive ('a man . . . shall cleave unto his wife: and they shall be one flesh'), and the later, that it is procreative ('be fruitful and multiply'), while the New Testament mentions a unitive and analogical purpose, but not expressly a procreative. Jewish and Christian traditions agree, however, in regarding the latter as the chief end of marriage, though for very different reasons. To the Jew the preservation of the family by securing a continuance of the male line from generation to generation was a necessity to which all other considerations were subordinated. Hence the permission of polygyny and of divorce for barrenness, and the desperate expedient of the levirate. The early

[1] See Foerster on *ktisis* in the *Theologisches Wörterbuch . . .*, ed. Kittel.

Christian view was quite different. With the accession of a personal hope the immortality which a man achieved in his descendants no longer mattered. The importance of the family diminished, and marriage came to be treated as inferior to virginity. In dealing with sexual activity the governing consideration in Patristic thought was really this: When is it permissible?—and the conclusion was that only an intention to procreate fully excused intercourse, which otherwise always involved, as we have seen, the commission of venial sin. The inference that procreation was the first end of marriage was thus inevitable; it was the only excuse for intercourse, and intercourse was only permissible between the married. At first the tendency was to restrict the sexual act to procreation,[1] but Augustine held that it was allowable for the satisfaction of the lust which proceeds from incontinence, and that marriage guarded husband and wife from adultery and fornication.[2] To procreation, therefore, another, secondary end of marriage was added; it was a remedy against sin. Augustine, however, treats less of the ends than of the blessings of marriage, and his threefold classification of these was universally accepted in the West until the time of the Reformation. These *bona matrimonii* were 'offspring' (which included not only the begetting and bearing of the child, but its being 'lovingly welcomed, kindly nourished, religiously brought up'); 'faith', or fidelity to the partner in marriage; and 'sacrament', or the signification of the union.[3]

According to the *Summa Theologica*, marriage is primarily an office of nature,[4] and as such has two ends—a principal end, which is the good of the offspring, and a secondary end:

. . . the mutual services which married persons render one another in household matters.[5]

[1] Cf. Athenagoras, *Legat.*, xxxiii.
[2] *de bono conj.*, vi; cf. the pseudo-Clementine *Homilies*, iii. 68, and *Ep. ad Jacob.*, vii.
[3] *de bono conj.*, xxiv; cf. *de Gen. ad litt.*, ix.
[4] III Supp. xlii 2 ad 2.   [5] III Supp. xli 1 *resp.*

These together constitute its essential final cause, to which can be added the accidental final cause—that is, what the contracting parties intend shall result from their union.[1] Over and above this, marriage between Christians is a sacrament of the Church; it is

> . . . a sanctifying remedy against sin offered to man under sensible signs.[2]

Since marriage involves a loss of reason due to pleasure, and to the tribulation of the flesh caused by solicitude for temporal things,[3] it receives as compensations the blessings enumerated by Augustine. The first (offspring), by ensuring the continuance of the species, fulfils a double purpose in securing the good of the state and the perpetuation of the Church.[4] The third (sacrament) implies, not only the indissolubility of the marriage union,[5] but also

> . . . all things that result from marriage being a sign of Christ's union with the Church.[6]

The relative importance of the three *bona* varies, since they can be considered in terms either of essentiality or of excellence. The blessing of sacrament is in every way the most excellent and, if the blessings are considered in themselves, the most essential too, because

> . . . there is no matrimony without inseparability, whereas there is matrimony without faith and offspring, because the existence of a thing does not depend upon its use.

If, however, the blessings are considered with reference to their principles (so that offspring denotes the intention of having children, and faith the duty of fidelity), first offspring, and then faith, are more essential and therefore more important

---

[1] III Supp. xlviii 2 *resp.*   [2] III Supp. xlii 1 *resp.*; cf. III lxi 1 and lxv 1.
[3] III Supp. xlix 1 *resp.*   [4] *Summa contra Gentiles*, iv. 78.
[5] *ibid.*; *Summa Theol.*, III Supp. xlix 2 ad 7.   [6] *ibid.*, 2 ad 4.

than sacrament, for without them there can be no matrimony, and to express in the marriage contract anything contrary to them would invalidate the union.[1]

The Anglican Reformers replaced the three *bona matrimonii* by three 'causes for which matrimony was ordained':

> One cause was the procreacion of children, to be brought vp in the feare and nurture of the Lorde, and prayse of God. Secondly it was ordeined for a remedie against sinne, and to auoyde fornycacion, that suche persons as be maryed, might liue chastly in matrimonie, and kepe themselfes vndefiled membres of Christes body. Thirdely for the mutuall societie, helpe and comfort, that the one ought to haue of the other, both in prosperitie and aduersitie.[2]

These causes, however, do not appear until the first Prayer Book sets them forth, and the Henrician formularies mark a transitional stage. *The Institution of a Christian Man* enumerates 'three special benefits or offices' belonging to matrimony: its signification (which implies avoidance of fornication), its indissolubility (which implies mutual fidelity), and

> ... the good and virtuous education and bringing up of the children begotten in the same.[3]

The resemblance to the three *bona* is more obvious in the reactionary 'King's Book', which mentions 'three good things' specially commended in marriage and describes the third as

> ... the child that cometh of marriage, and the good and virtuous education and bringing up of the same.[4]

[1] *ibid.*, III Supp. xlix 3 *resp.*
[2] Prayer Book of 1549 (F. E. Brightman, *The English Rite*, ii, p. 800–2); in 1661 an alteration was made in the second cause: '... that such persons as have not the gift of Continency, might marry, and keep themselves. ...'
[3] *Formularies of Faith* ..., pp. 89–92.
[4] *A Necessary Doctrine and Erudition for any Christian Man, Formularies of Faith* ..., pp. 275–7.

It is difficult to determine whether the order of the causes in the Prayer Book indicates their relative importance, or whether it is simply enumerative. It is generally understood that, being stated first, procreation is the primary end of marriage, but it is worth noting that the Prayer Book order receives support only from the abortive *Reformatio Legum Ecclesiasticarum*.[1] The most common order is: society, procreation, remedy. This may perhaps be implied by Hooper when he writes:

> Matrimony is a lawful conjunction of man and woman to be one flesh, to bring forth children, either to avoid fornication,[2]

and is followed in the Homily, *Of the State of Matrimony*, which teaches that marriage is

> . . . instituted of God to the intent that man and woman should live lawfully in a perpetual friendship, to bring forth fruit, and to avoid fornication.

Thomas Becon, in *The Booke of Matrimony*,[3] and Sandys, in a sermon preached at a wedding in Strasburg,[4] both give the causes in this order, while Bucer stated in the *Censura* that in his view the third cause ought to be placed first,[5] as being, in the words of Cosin's note,

> . . . the chiefest and most general cause for which marriage was ordained, even in paradise, *Faciamus in adjutorium*; but

[1] *de matrimonio*, cap. 1 (ed. Cardwell, p. 39): 'Matrimonium est legitimus contractus . . . in quo tradit uterque alteri potestatem sui corporis vel ad prolem suscipiendam, vel ad scortationem evitandam, vel ad vitam mutuis officiis gubernandam.'

[2] *A Declaration of the Ten Commandments*, x, *Works* (Parker Society), i, p. 381. It is very improbable that by putting first 'to be one flesh' Hooper desired to emphasize the primacy of the unitive end of marriage; nevertheless, he unconsciously bears testimony to an important principle.

[3] Part iii, *Works*, folio ed., i, fol. DCxlviii recto, ff.

[4] *Sermon* xvi, *Works* (Parker Society), p. 315.

[5] C. Hopf, *Martin Bucer and the English Reformation* (Oxford, 1946), p. 72.

they thought it better to let it stand as it was; for society and help may be had without marriage . . . but procreation of children cannot lawfully be had without it.[1]

Jeremy Taylor also regarded society as the principal purpose of marriage, and procreation as its second purpose; avoidance of fornication, he says,

. . . came in by the superfoetation of the evil accidents of the world.[2]

Tyndale[3] and Donne,[4] on the other hand, considered that the chief end of marriage was the provision of a remedy against sin, and relegated society to the third place.

It is evident that among the Anglican divines of the sixteenth and seventeenth centuries procreation was not accepted as the principal end of marriage, and little importance was attached to the order in which the Prayer Book states the causes for which matrimony was ordained—which may indicate that the order itself was looked upon merely as one of enumeration. Later on, however, opinion tended to revert to the traditional view, though Kingsley, who held that the unique love between husband and wife is indestructible even by death, wrote thus of the question put to Jesus by the Sadducees concerning marriage and the resurrection:

I leave all in the hands of a good God; and can so far trust His Son Jesus Christ Our Lord, as to be sure that he knew the best method of protesting against the old Jewish error (which Popish casuists still formally assert) that the first end of marriage is the procreation of children, and thereby laid the true foundation for the emancipation of woman. . . .[5]

1 *Notes on the Book of Common Prayer*, series III, *Works* (Lib. of Angl.-Cath. Theol.), v, p. 492.
2 *Sermons*, xvii (*The Marriage Ring*, pt. 1), *Works*, iv, p. 215.
3 *The Obedience of a Christian Man, Works* (Parker Society), i, p. 254.
4 *Sermons*, lxxxiii, *Works* (1839), iv, p. 33.
5 *Letters and Memories*, ii, p. 103.

Kingsley was not an outstanding theologian, but his ideas on marriage deserve more attention than they have received.

In the description of marriage as a 'remedy against sin' two ideas meet—the first, that only between husband and wife is sexual activity legitimate and to be excused; the second, that being a sacrament, marriage is a 'healing remedy' against the sin of concupiscence, by which the grace of temperance is conveyed.[1] Since marriage was not recognized as a sacrament in the Thomist sense, either by the compilers of the Prayer Book or by the Anglicanism which they represented, it can only be assumed that the second 'cause' in the rites of 1549, 1552, 1559, and 1661 refers simply to the fact that marriage does undoubtedly afford a legitimate sphere for sex activity to those who cannot contain—though it would not, of course, have been denied that, being a state of life ordained by God, the Christian receives grace to live worthily therein. The phrase 'a remedy against sin' has, however, proved offensive to modern taste; hence the revised Prayer Book of 1928 substitutes a statement that marriage was instituted

. . . in order that the natural instincts and affections, implanted by God, should be hallowed and directed aright; that those who are called of God to this holy estate, should continue therein in pureness of living,

while the 1929 Scottish Prayer Book solves the difficulty by the convenient but not altogether satisfactory expedient of omission.

There are several objections against defining marriage as a remedy against sin. Though it has ancient authority, it is doubtful whether such an idea would have arisen or gained currency in the absence of the negative, evasive attitude to sex so characteristic of early Christianity. It is not to be denied that marriage prevents or reduces unregulated and promiscuous sex activity in sinful man by diverting it into channels

[1] Cf. *Summa Theol.*, III lxi 1 *resp.*; lxv 1 *resp.*; III Supp. xlii 1 *sed contra*.

which have the approval of religion and society; nor that marriage is the only context in which that activity can properly conform to God's will. But the union of husband and wife is not happily described as, among other things, a divinely appointed means for the avoidance of fornication; the implication is that for all who have not the gift of continence, the sexual urge is so uncontrollable as to make marriage the only alternative to irregular intercourse, but experience does not confirm this. Not only is the idea of 'remedy' negative, but it suggests also a low view of the dignity of marriage which, as the Prayer Book distinctly says, ought not to be entered for the satisfaction of 'men's carnal lusts and affections'; indeed, to marry simply because of incontinence would be immoral. And since matrimony is expressly stated to have been 'instituted of God in the time of man's innocency', it is open to question whether it is not quite inaccurate to assert that it was 'ordained' as a 'remedy against sin'—unless the view be taken that it was so ordained in anticipation of the foreseen fact of the Fall.

While it may be explained and even defended, this 'cause' is capable of serious misunderstanding, and introduces an undesirable note into the Service. The substitution made in the 1928 English revision of the Prayer Book is to be commended; it is less offensive, and has positive value in that it recognizes sex as a gift of God, and marriage as a vocation. But the sinfulness of fornication and adultery needs to be vigorously and uncompromisingly stated, preferably in the opening exhortation; this is an addition that the times demand.

Despite the contrary tradition in classic Anglicanism, the primacy of the procreative end of marriage still remains a basic principle in theology and in jurisprudence, and is generally held to rest upon the natural law itself. It may readily be conceded that the chief purpose of marriage as a social institution is the continuance of the species; it is, as Lacey says, a

... permanent connexion of man and woman for the purpose
of producing and raising children.[1]

But marriage possesses more than a merely biological or social
significance, as Augustine and the Schoolmen perceived. The
natural law, which is invoked in support of the traditional
view, suggests from another standpoint that the primary end
of marriage is *unitive* and not procreative—that its principal
purpose must be sought on the ontological plane, in all that is
meant by the metaphysical *henosis* of 'one flesh' which is
established through sexual union.

As we have already seen, Scripture says little about the
primacy of the procreative end of marriage. The injunction,
'be fruitful and multiply', which belongs to the later, priestly
stratum of Genesis, is addressed once to mankind generally,
and three times to the Patriarchs Noah and Jacob;[2] it is typical
of the Hebrew's concern for a large number of children, and
cannot be construed as implying that the sole or even the chief
end of marriage is generation. On the other hand, the importance which Jesus and St. Paul attach to Gen. 2.24 suggests
that the establishment of the 'one flesh' union is the first
purpose for which men and women are brought together by
God. Nowhere in the New Testament is any prominence
assigned to procreation,[3] whereas the great Pauline conception
of marriage as the analogue of Christ's union with His Church
is indisputably unitive. It is of course arguable that the primacy
of the procreative end is too obvious to need any emphasis, but
the prominence given to the idea of union in 'one flesh' is too
great to be explained simply as an attempt to establish the
importance of a new but secondary end of marriage.

In Christian, though not in Jewish tradition, the notion
that procreation is the principal end of marriage is connected

---

[1] Lacey-Mortimer, *op. cit.*, p. 3 (original ed., pp. 3-4).

[2] Gen. 1.28, 9.1,7, 35.11.

[3] It has been held that I Tim. 5.14 teaches that offspring is the purpose of
marriage, but on entirely insufficient grounds.

closely with the view that procreation is the sole purpose of, and justification for, sexual intercourse. But generation, as we have already noticed, is only one of the functions of sex. Moreover, intercourse has no exclusive connexion with procreation, though that alone may be its biological end; it does not always result in conception, it can take place during pregnancy and menstruation, and is satisfactorily possible after a woman's childbearing days are over. And when the delicate and complicated organization of human sexuality is considered, it becomes difficult to explain it, or to explain it away, in terms of generation alone. It seems perfectly clear, as Brunner says,[1] that

. . . the Christian ethic must stand for the independent meaning of the erotic and sex element within marriage as an expression of love, not merely as a means of procreation.

—and it has been shown that sex has other non-procreative functions apart from the expression of love.

Since it is as a sexual union established and sustained by sexual intercourse that marriage is distinguished from every other kind of legitimate relation or partnership between man and woman, the purpose of sex must inevitably determine to no small extent the purpose of marriage itself. It must not be overlooked, therefore, that sexual intercourse, whether or not it results in conception, always has profound consequences in the realm of personal relation. The 'one flesh' *henosis* is not merely a by-product of a biological function. Marriage derives its ontological meaning, not from the procreative capacity of husband and wife, but from the sexual love by which they are united in a special and significant personal relation. Intercourse may imply the possibility of procreation, but it means the certainty of union in 'one flesh'.

May we say, then, that marriage has different, rather than primary and secondary, ends?—that its chief institutional (and

[1] *The Divine Imperative*, p. 368.

biological) purpose is procreation; that in relation to the personal life its first object is integration and fulfilment; and that ontologically its unitive end is primary. This would at least be more satisfactory than the traditional method of attempting to arrange certain acceptable ends in the order of their supposed importance, but it is open to one objection. It fails to distinguish between the essential and the accidental in marriage, and does not sufficiently emphasize that its distinctive element is the *henosis* of man and woman in 'one flesh'. In regard to its ends, as in other respects, marriage must be assessed primarily as a personal relation, and with reference to its ontological character—and this leads inevitably to the conclusion (which Scripture supports) that its principal purpose is unitive. It must be made clear that this does not imply any minimizing of the importance of procreation, although it cannot any longer be accepted as the chief end of marriage. The purpose of the foregoing reconsideration has been to show that the first purpose for which God calls men and women together is that they may become 'one flesh'; it has not been to depreciate the first cause 'for which matrimony was ordained'. The unitive end of marriage takes precedence over the procreative end simply because it stands in a closer relation than the latter to the essential nature of the *henosis*, and since it does so by virtue of Divine ordination, no contravention of any principle of natural law is involved.

IX

THE ANALOGICAL SIGNIFICANCE OF UNION IN 'ONE FLESH'

ST. PAUL, in the Epistle to the Ephesians,[1] first referred to the symbolical or analogical importance of the 'one flesh' union, and the Marriage Service, following him, declares that God has

[1] Eph. 5.22–33.

. . . consecrated the state of Matrimony to such an excellent mystery, that in it is signified and represented the spiritual marriage and unity betwixt Christ and his Church.

He did not elaborate this idea, and apart from a few pregnant suggestions, it has had comparatively little influence upon the theology of marriage. Reflection upon all that it implies, however, serves to confirm Jeremy Taylor's view that marriage is

. . . the symbolical and sacramental representment of the greatest mysteries of our religion,[1]

and it is now proposed to consider the whole subject more fully.

In each of these mysteries—Christ and the Church, the Incarnation, the Trinity, and others—an eternal principle of unity is involved, which cannot adequately be grasped by the mind, still less expressed in words. Any attempt to explain the mystery of God's triunity must necessarily be imperfect, and even so, intelligible only to the educated—perhaps only to the trained theologian or philosopher. Yet man is constantly dependent upon and brought into relation with the Blessed Trinity, while the life of the Christian centres in the mysteries which are the signs of the invasion of time by the Eternal. He lives by these mysteries, but he needs also to try to comprehend them—yet where in human experience is he to find anything comparable, for example, to the Divine triunity?—for he can only express his insights by means of analogy and symbolism. He can, of course, find nothing strictly comparable to the eternal pattern of complete union without loss of distinction, but by contemplating the mystery of marriage, and by becoming himself 'one flesh' with another, he can penetrate as deeply as his finite limitations allow into the great mysteries of the Faith.

In their metaphysical *henosis* in marriage man and woman

[1] *Sermons*, xvii (*The Marriage Ring*, pt. 1), *Works*, iv, p. 212.

become 'one', yet they lose none of their personal autonomy or distinction. Their biune relation, as we have emphasized, is quite unlike any other human association or relation, and affords the simplest and most apposite analogue to the mysteries of the Trinity, the Incarnation, and the Church. It is the best finite exemplification of union without confusion or loss of distinction. Although the analogue must at best be imperfect, it gains force from personal experience; to those who are truly 'one flesh' their unity is no sentimental figure of speech, but a real if ineffable fact. Indeed, not only do they feel and know that they are 'one', but somehow they communicate a sense of their singleness. But the validity of the analogies rests upon the inner character of the *henosis*, and does not stand or fall by subjective proof or evidence.

Augustine hints at, but does not follow up the analogy between the Trinity and the 'one flesh' biunity. He argues that man was made in the image of God, but not woman; she, therefore,

> . . . together with her own husband is the image of God, so that the whole substance [that is, the *henosis*] may be one image.

He rightly rejects the idea that the father-mother-child relation is a figure of the Trinity; those who said it was seem to have thought that the man represented the Father, the mother the Spirit, and the child the Son.[1] Here the analogy must not be pressed; marriage affords no parallel to the eternal generation of the Son, nor to the eternal procession of the Holy Spirit. Doms, it is true, claims that the procreation of a child is an imperfect reflection of the generation of the Son,[2] but he disregards the exclusive character of the *henosis*, to which the child bears no ontological relation and is strictly accidental. For the same reason the idea that the birth of a child corresponds to the procession of the Spirit must be rejected.

[1] *de Trin.*, xii. 5–8.   [2] *The Meaning of Marriage*, p. 18.

The essence of the analogy between the 'one flesh' union and the Trinity consists in the fact that both involve personal relation. In the *henosis* God's nature as a Divine society is reflected; as Father and Son are united by the Spirit in a bond of love, and as the coinherent life of the three Persons is a life of love exchanged, so husband and wife are also united by a distinctive tie of love, and live as 'one flesh' a life founded upon the exchange of love.

Doms pursues further the idea of man and woman in their sexual union as types of the Persons of the Trinity by discussing the creation of the first man and woman:

The first man appeared as the image of the Father (*imago Patris*) and likeness of the Son (*similitudo Filii*): the first woman as likeness of the Holy Spirit (*similitudo Spiritus Sancti*).

This, he says,

. . . corresponds rather better to the Greek conception of the Trinity—the production of the Holy Ghost 'through' the Son. It opens the way to the beautiful and profound thought that, just as God performs all his outside (*ad extra*) works *through* (*per*) his Word, *in* the Spirit of his Love, so he makes use of his likeness to propagate and multiply the image of his nature immanent in human nature.[1]

There are distinct affinities between these ideas and those of Augustine.

The Pauline analogy between marriage and Christ's union with His Church is heightened by the parallel subordination-ism[2] displayed in the two relations:

. . . the husband is the head of the wife, as Christ also is the head of the Church.

[1] *The Meaning of Marriage*, pp. 16–17.
[2] See Appendix II on St. Paul's idea of Subordination.

From this follow the obligations and responsibilities of dual submission (from above and from below):

> . . . as the church is subject to Christ, so let the wives also be to their husbands in everything. Husbands, love your wives, even as Christ also loved the church, and gave himself up for it. . . .[1]

Only in marriage can true subordination and superordination be set forth adequately in terms of human relation; only in marriage too can the love of Christ, most notably expressed in His self-giving for the Church, be exemplified in terms of human love—in the husband's love for his wife as for his own body. And in Christian marriage there is more than symbolism, for in the common life of the husband and wife who are 'one flesh' in Christ there is embodied

> . . . the divine-human *koinonia* of God and man in Christ. It [marriage] is to be an 'effectual sign' of that divine-human *koinonia*, the earthly union being engraced with the graces which abound in the heavenly union.[2]

There are naturally many allusions in Christian theology to this Pauline analogy, but few are more than quotation or comment. Among the more curious is the view of Leo the Great that as by the regulation that the Levitical priest must marry a virgin[3] the spiritual marriage between Christ and the Church was prefigured, so by the Christian priest being the 'husband of one wife' it is truly exemplified.[4] One of the most profound ideas in this connexion, however, appears in *The Union of Christ and the Church; in a Shadow* by the Cambridge Platonist Ralph Cudworth, who argues that the union of man and woman in marriage does not constitute simply a 'bare similitude' of the mystical union, nor yet an accidental likeness, but that the human relation is a divinely appointed image or copy of the

---

[1] Eph. 5.23–5.
[2] L. S. Thornton, *The Common Life in the Body of Christ*, p. 225.
[3] Lev. 21.13.   [4] *Epist.* xii,3.

heavenly, spiritual relation. Christ and the Church are *sponsus et sponsa archetypi*, and husband and wife *sponsus et sponsa ectypi*.[1] This suggests that the 'one flesh' union may have been ordained by God expressly to show forth intelligibly to men the truth, not only about this, but about the other mysteries of the Christian Faith. Having revealed them to us, He provided us with the key to their meaning.

The mysterious *henosis* of husband and wife symbolizes also the union of the risen and glorified Christ with the sacramental elements of bread and wine in the Eucharist. Doms points out the significant parallel between the Communion and the act of intercourse:

> . . . in both [the marital and the Christ/Church relations] the mysterious unity of husband and wife is realized through their participation in an act of the body which somehow enables them to share each other's vital forces. Physical participation in the giving of the whole Christ is the foundation of the life of the Church; the personal giving of husband and wife to each other, and the *physical* realization of this giving in the marriage act, mark the highest point of attainment in their participation in the life of each other.[2]

Again, the *henosis* exemplifies the union of God and man in one Christ. The Son of Man took His human nature from the womb of a woman in order to establish among men the union formally realized in Baptism and the Eucharist, just as woman herself was taken from man's side in order to make marital union possible.[3]

The Incarnation is often described as a marriage. For example, Origen says,

> More truly indeed of this [the union of the Word with human nature] than of any other [union] can the statement

[1] See J. Tulloch, *Rational Theology . . . in England in the Seventeenth Century*, ii, pp. 200–1.
[2] *op. cit.*, p. 103.　　[3] *ibid.*, p. 114.

be affirmed, 'They shall both be in one flesh, and are no longer two, but one flesh'. For the Word of God is to be considered as being more in one flesh with the soul [of Jesus] than a man with his wife.[1]

And again, referring to the union of the Word with human nature, he writes:

... the sacred language of Holy Scripture knows of other things also, which, although 'dual' in their own nature, are considered to be, and really are, 'one' in respect to one another. It is said of husband and wife, 'They are no longer twain, but one flesh'. ...[2]

Cassian understands the *mega mustērion* of Eph. 5.32 to refer to the Incarnation,[3] and Augustine interprets the union of husband and wife in 'one flesh' as an analogue of the marriage between God and man:

The nuptial union is that of the Word and the flesh; the Bridechamber of this union, the Virgin's womb. For the flesh itself was united to the Word: whence also it is said, 'Henceforth they are not twain, but one flesh'.[4]

The same idea appears in Anglican formularies[5] and writings; Taylor, for instance, says:

Christ descended from His Father's bosom, and contracted His divinity with flesh and blood, and married our nature, and we became a church, the spouse of the Bridegroom. ...[6]

Marriage thus affords the best finite analogue to the mysterious *henosis* effected once for all 'not by confusion of substance, but

---

[1] *de princ.*, ii. 4.   [2] *contra Celsum*, vi. 47.   [3] *de incarn. Dom. contra Nest.*, v. 12.
[4] *Hom. in Ps.*, *xlv*, 3; see also *Hom. in Joh.*, viii. 4; *Hom. in 1 Joh.*, i. 2; *Hom. in Ps. xix*, exp. ii.6.
[5] *The Institution of a Christian Man* (*Formularies* . . ., p. 84); *A Necessary Doctrine* . . . (*Formularies* . . ., p. 271).
[6] *Sermons*, xvii (*The Marriage Ring*, pt. 1), *Works*, iv, p. 212.

by unity of Person'. The subordination of woman to man in the unity of 'one flesh' also suggests the relation between the human and the Divine in Christ.[1]

Both Christian and non-Christian mystics have described the relation between God and the soul in nuptial terms, and in this connexion sexual intercourse has special significance:

> Two persons, through a specific act, participate in each other's being without losing their autonomy,

and their union thus constitutes

> . . . the most profound natural analogy of our own participation in God's nature

through sanctifying grace.[2]

The 'one flesh' *henosis* exemplifies also the unity which underlies the phenomenal multiplicity in the universe—that unity which has its source in the creative will of God and is implied in the creative activity of the Word. Thus it points forward to the eschatological consummation when God will 'sum up all things in Christ', and so accomplish the mysterious purpose of which St. Paul writes to the Ephesians.

Further, in the unity attained by husband and wife as 'one flesh' the ideal unity of the whole human race is foreshadowed:

> . . . in marriage individuals are the almost passive instruments of a force which is above and beyond them, which is in them but not for them, and which, by making use of them as instruments, does more than they themselves do. It is the human race which acts in them, thus insofar as is possible for it, by that activity declaring, establishing, and fulfilling itself; realizing its unity and completeness in individuals, and not in itself, for in itself it has no independent being.[3]

---

[1] See, on this section, also C. Chavasse, *The Bride of Christ*, pp. 151-4, etc.
[2] Doms, *op. cit.*, p. 99.
[3] E. Mersch, *Love, Marriage, and Chastity* (trans. A. B., London, 1939), pp. 8-9. See also the note to pp. 12-16 on the partial realization in marriage of the ideal dynamic unity of the human race.

This unity is to be achieved on the physical level through the transcending of all barriers of race, colour, language, culture, and class, and on the spiritual level in the gathering together of all men in Christ as members of an undivided and truly catholic Church—for, as Augustine wrote, marriage signifies

> . . . the unity of us all made subject to God, which shall be hereafter in one heavenly City.[1]

It stands for that fundamental unity of all Christians in Christ which goes deeper than their divisions, and emphasizes, against denominational and sectarian cleavages, the oneness of all believers for which Jesus prayed.

The *henosis* of man and woman, each the diametrical opposite of the other, is the symbol of what love could do towards the healing of those divisions from which humanity and the Church suffer so grievously.

For husband and wife the importance of the signification of their union lies in the responsibility which it reveals. Vocation to marriage is above all vocation to exemplify analogically to the world, through a dedicated common life, the nature of the Christian mysteries and the eternal truth of union without loss of distinction. This also emphasizes the primacy of the unitive end of marriage; children or none, the two-in-'one flesh' union must declare the triunity of God, and the love which is ontologically the foundation of the *henosis* must reflect that mutual exchange of love which eternally unites the three Persons in the Divine society. Thus marriage has an evangelistic purpose which cannot be evaded, for by its means alone can the nature of unity be made known; this is another and very weighty reason why it is not to be 'enterprized, nor taken in hand, unadvisedly, lightly, or wantonly'. Every marriage failure is a failure to respond to the calling of God, and to proclaim the meaning of unity, and a further contribution to the sum total of human division.

[1] *de bono conj.*, xviii [21].

X

PROCREATION AND THE FAMILY

THE analogy between the 'one flesh' union and the Trinity must not be pressed beyond the proper limits of analogy. The inescapable contingency of the *henosis* means that, in and by itself, it can never enjoy that sufficiency of life which God in Trinity enjoys as a Divine society. For Him, creation is not a necessity; for husband and wife it is integral to their very existence. As individuals, they are under a mysterious internal compulsion to seek personal completion through sexual union; as two united in 'one flesh' they seek to enrich the life of the *henosis* by building around it a small society through procreation, not accretion.

The creative need felt by man and woman is first satisfied by the establishment of the *henosis*:

Lovemaking—and with it the whole common life of work and play and thought and speech and prayer—is the first act of husband and wife as creators. Together they create through these things the first new thing, the unity of the two-in-one.[1]

This is the general creative purpose of sex, but it has also a specific creative purpose—procreation—wherein those who are married co-operate with God in furthering the life of the race and of the Church. In fulfilling this great purpose they do not surrender their autonomy and abandon themselves to the impulse of some instinctive natural urge, but freely and responsibly participate in the Divine work. They may thus determine the end of any one sexual act so as to include or exclude the possibility of conception, but may not determine the end of their total sexual activity so as to deny its procreative purpose. They must recognize in the impulse to sexual union a creative

[1] Gerald Vann in *Blackfriars*, xxiii, No. 266 (May, 1942), p. 171.

element which seeks fulfilment both in the establishment of the 'one flesh' *henosis* and in bringing new life into existence.

The *henosis* is ontologically complete, but socially imperfect, and needs to be supplemented from outside itself if it is to attain to fullness of interior life. Fellowship with other men and women can mean a valuable enrichment of the 'one flesh', and husband and wife must take care not to sever themselves from the social life of the community by retiring into the secure and impenetrable retreat of their own secret union. It will, however, always be in the children who are uniquely their creation and the expression of their love in its complete self-giving, rather than in their friends, that they find their true and most satisfactory social fulfilment, even though the *henosis* must always remain something within but apart from the family, something to which the child is strictly extraneous.

The blessing of children, therefore, is rather of the *bene esse* than the *esse*, as it were, of life as 'one flesh'. Sexual intercourse may be fruitful in establishing and sustaining the union of husband and wife, in completing and integrating them as persons, and yet not be fruitful in the specific sense of leading to conception and birth. In such a case the social orbit of the *henosis* must be expanded by other means, for the two cannot live to themselves alone. But when children come to satisfy their creative desire, they can expend upon them the love which overflows the limits of the primary relation and demands an object upon which to pour itself out creatively.

Though the family and the 'one flesh' *henosis* are not identical the latter is the nucleus around which the family is built, and the source from which it draws its vitality. The child is necessarily extraneous to the *henosis*, which is a specific, exclusive union of man and woman, but he can be given a share in its life; this is analogous to man's participation in eternal life through grace, though not by right. Marriage ought to mean, therefore, a vocation to establish a life in 'one flesh' of such integrity and vitality that it can be shared with the

children and will permeate the family with its spirit. From the *henosis* as its nucleus the family derives its essential meaning. Sociologically it may simply be regarded as a basic group of related individuals, an extension of marriage in its institutional aspect. Theologically, however, it is in some sense an extension of the 'one flesh' *henosis*, a distinctive community to which the nucleus gives significance and a certain metaphysical unity. The family is 'one' as husband and wife are 'one'; this does not depend upon a crude, materialistic idea of 'blood-unity' any more than the *henosis* depends upon the crude fact of physical intercourse. The common 'blood' and the sexual union are symbols and expressions of a profound metaphysical and spiritual relation.

As an extension of the 'one flesh' *henosis* the family reflects some of its characteristics. There is the same complete sharing of a common life, for there is no true family where some members hold themselves aloof, claiming both the right to live their own lives and the right to a place within the circle, sharing the life which emanates from the centre. But in every direction the interior intensity and exclusiveness of marriage is modified in the family; as a type of human community it stands midway between the *henosis* and such loosely-knit associations as the state, which have no organic unity or character. The contingency of its relation to society is therefore less strongly marked, and its tragic character less pronounced; the same sort of tension is less likely to arise. Like marriage, it involves acceptance of the principle of subordination;[1] there must be both unilateral submission of children to parents, and submission by all, one to another, in love.

The family also has its analogical significance. In it are exemplified the Fatherhood of God 'from whom all fatherhood in heaven and earth is named',[2] and the sonship of the redeemed who are 'led by the Spirit of God'.[3] Parents, accordingly, are charged with the responsibility of displaying the loving care,

---

[1] See Appendix II.   [2] Eph. 3.14–15.   [3] Rom. 8.14.

patience, and impartiality of the eternal Father, and children in their turn must show the loyalty, obedience, trust, and responsiveness of the true son of God, and especially of Him who perfectly did the Father's will and glorified Him by His obedience even unto the death of the Cross. Finally, the family is a little Church, a microcosm of the Body of Christ, and must manifest by its *koinōnia* the church-like quality of its life.

XI

SECOND MARRIAGE AND THE IDEA OF 'ONE FLESH'

SECOND marriage—that is, remarriage after the death of a partner—was the subject of some discussion in early times. According to the Pastoral Epistles, deacons, *presbuteroi* and *episkopoi* must be husbands 'of one wife',[1] but it is very doubtful whether these injunctions were directed against second marriages among the clergy.[2] Eventually, however, they came to be regarded as Apostolic prohibitions excluding from the ministry those who had married again after the death of a first wife.[3] In the East an exception was made; only two or more marriages *after baptism* disqualified a man for ordination,[4] but no such distinction was recognized in the West.[5] Some were opposed to this strict interpretation of 'the husband of one wife'; Callistus is alleged not to have degraded clergy who had

[1] I Tim. 3.2, 12; Tit. 1.6.

[2] See W. Lock, *The Pastoral Epistles* (Int. Crit. Comm.), pp. 36-8.

[3] See *Test. Dom. N. J. Christi*, i. 20; Tertullian, *ad ux.*, i. 7; Clem. Alex., *Strom*, iii. 12; Origen, *Hom. xvii in Luc.*; *Apostolical Constitutions*, ii. 2 and vi. 17; *Apostolic Canons*, 17 (16); Chrysostom, *Hom. in Tit.*, ii. 1, prohibiting ordination to the priesthood of one who had married a second time; Basil, *Epist.* clxxxviii *ad Ampliochium*, 12.

[4] This was amended, however, at the Quinisext (Trullan) Council, can. 3.

[5] cf. *Conc. Valent. Gall.*, I (374), can. 1; *Conc. Agath.* (506), can. 1; see also Augustine, *de bono conj.*, xviii (21), who says the matter is one 'of sacrament, not of sin'.

married twice or even three times,[1] and Theodore of Mopsuestia considered it ridiculous to hold that St. Paul's rule
excluded any man of virtuous life who happened to have contracted a second marriage after baptism—he was of the opinion
that it simply disqualified those who had at any time practised
synchronous polygyny or concubinage, or who had been
unfaithful to their marriage vows.[2]

Second marriage among the laity was not at first looked
upon with disapproval, and St. Paul actually recommends the
young widows to marry.[3] Hermas, however, considered it
meritorious to refrain from taking another partner after the
death of a first.[4] According to the *Apostolical Constitutions*, to
marry once is righteous; second marriage is allowable to
young widows as a protection; third marriage is an indication
of incontinence; and marriages beyond the third are

> . . . manifest fornication and unquestionable uncleanness.[5]

Cyril of Jerusalem held that second marriage was permissible
in order that the weak may not fall into fornication.[6] Chrysostom regarded it as a thing 'liable to many ill constructions';
although he is careful to make it clear that St. Paul does not
allow him to pronounce it a proof of wantonness, he refers, in
almost the same breath, to the women who

> . . . enter into a second marriage and defile the bed of their
> deceased husband, though they have loved him.[7]

This curious vein of sentimentality reappears in a discussion
of the Pauline injunction concerning the bishop:

> . . . he who retains no kind regard for her who is departed,
> how shall he be a good president?[8]

---

[1] See Hippolytus, *Philosopheuma*, ix. 12.
[2] *Comm. in Ep. ad Tim. I, ad loc.*; see H. B. Swete, *Theodore of Mopsuestia on the Minor Epistles of S. Paul*, ii, pp. 99–108.
[3] I Tim. 5.14.   [4] *Mand.*, iv. 4.   [5] iii. 2.
[6] *Cat. Lect.*, iv. 26.   [7] *Hom. in Epist. II ad Tim.*, vii. 4.
[8] Chrysostom, *Hom. in Epist. ad Tit.*, ii. 1.

Ambrose permitted, but did not recommend second marriage, and disapproved of repeated unions.[1] Augustine; too, was moderate in his view of the matter; he censured the opinions of the Novatians, Tertullian, and the Montanists, but insisted that widowhood was more honourable than second marriage.[2]

A more extreme attitude is represented by Gregory Nazianzen, who wrote:

> The first [marriage] is law, the second is indulgence, the third is transgression, and anything beyond this is swinish.[3]

Athenagoras termed second marriage 'specious adultery', and seemed to regard a husband as still bound to the deceased wife:

> . . . he who deprives himself of his first wife, even though she be dead, is a cloaked adulterer.[4]

Tertullian even considered that it bordered upon fornication.[5] Those who married again after bereavement were sometimes suspended or made to undergo penance,[6] and one council debarred the widow of a bishop, priest, or deacon who remarried from eating with a cleric or religious woman, and would only admit her to Communion *in articulo mortis*.[7] This condemnation of second marriage as the miserable evidence of an incontinent or licentious disposition shows very clearly how perverted an idea of sex was current in some parts of the early Church.

By contrast, very little was said about the matter by either the Schoolmen or the Anglican divines. According to the *Summa Theologica*, second marriage has all the essentials of a sacrament and excuses the sexual act from sin even as a first marriage. Although, considered in itself, it is fully significant of the union between Christ and the Church, yet considered in

---

[1] *de vid.*, 68.   [2] *de bono vid.*, vi; cf *de bono conj.*, xxi.
[3] *Hom. in Matt. xix*, 8.   [4] *Legat.*, xxxiii.   [5] *de exhort. cast.*, ix.
[6] Basil, *Epist.* clxxxviii *ad Amplioch.*, 4; *Conc. Laodic.*, can. 1; *Conc. Neocesaren.*, can. 7.
[7] *Conc. Toletan.*, I, can. 18.

relation to the first marriage, it is defective in significance.[1]
Hardly any English writers of the sixteenth and seventeenth
centuries mention second marriage, and all who do assume that
it is entirely lawful and unobjectionable. Kingsley, however,
took a different and very characteristic view; while he did not
regard second marriage as sinful, he said that

> Lovers of high and pure minds now shrink from [it],
> because marriage is so spiritual and timeless—so pure and
> mysterious—an Eternal union, which once solemnized
> with the loved one can be transferred to no other—which
> death cannot part.[2]

He admitted that this opinion was 'peculiar', and allowed that
second marriages are permissible,[3]

> . . . but from the beginning it was not so, and will not be
> so, some day, when the might of love becomes generally
> appreciated.[4]

So long as propriety is observed, second marriage is usually
considered unexceptionable. Kingsley's objections were sentimental rather than theological, but Dr. Otto Piper's criticism
demands more serious consideration. He disapproves of
second marriage for two reasons. First, he says,

> . . . it would contradict the original model of the marriage
> of Christ with his Church.[5]

Here it would seem that the nuptial symbolism is pressed too
far and interpreted too literally. The heavenly Bridegroom has
only one Bride, admittedly, and the Church only one Head;
but a husband can only be in true relation with one (living)

---

[1] III Supp. lxiii 2.

[2] *Letters and Memories*, i, p. 151.

[3] 'They are no more sin to those who have not entered into the higher idea of marriage, than polygamy is sinful to the heathen . . .', *ibid*.

[4] *ibid*., ii, p. 106.   [5] *op. cit*., pp. 83–4.

wife, and a wife only with one (living) husband. The analogy is between the *union* of Christ with the Church and the 'one flesh' *henosis*; the one is permanent and indestructible, the other can be dissolved by death and constituted again by remarriage. Two successive *henoses*, therefore, can witness in turn to the mystery of which marriage is the analogue. The contradiction would only exist if a real *henosis* remained between a living husband and a dead wife, or a dead husband and a living wife.

Second, Dr. Piper claims that second marriage denies

. . . the exclusive character of the secret of sex.[1]

But though one who remarries understands the secret of sex, he understands it only as it has been revealed to him by his first partner—that is to say, his knowledge is particular and therefore limited. To 'know' one man or one woman is not to 'know' all men and women. In a second marriage, therefore, the new partner is the mediator or mediatrix of new knowledge. The initial act of 'knowing' must be unique simply because it is the first, but subsequent sexual knowledge is none the less authentic. Although one who remarries is aware that sexual experience conveys personal knowledge, he cannot know precisely what kind or degree of knowledge will be disclosed in the new act of 'knowing'. This will equally be true in those cases where both husband and wife have had previous sexual experience in marriage. In the 'one flesh' union, too, knowledge is always imparted as well as received, and where the second partner is a virgin, there is the unique first knowledge to impart.

[1] *op. cit.*, p. 162; see also p. 137.

APPENDIX I

LOVE AND PASSION

'PASSION' generally signifies intense sexual love, and often implies a subtle emphasis upon its physical aspect. But in *Passion and Society* Denis de Rougement treats love and passion as distinct and opposite ideas; for him, the latter is sexual experience sought because it involves frustration, suffering, and in the end death. He finds its origin in Manicheism, and claims that it was really the theme of the literature of Courtly Love.

His thesis is that the new love which appeared during the eleventh century originally had nothing to do with sexual relation, but was integrally connected with the Catharist heresy which then flourished in Provençe. Catharist mysticism was basically Manichean, and he suggests that Courtly Love was in fact nothing more than a symbol invented to express the flight of the soul from the world in order to achieve union with the divine love. It was thus a revival of the old Eros-mysticism, which regarded the soul as divine and so always striving to escape from the material form in which it had been imprisoned. This was described by means of a mythological dualism of light and darkness, expressed in sexual terms: the soul's yearning for 'light', or the divine, was 'symbolized by the nocturnal attraction of sex', and woman represented 'the other world, and the nostalgia which makes us despise earthly joys'.[1] Hence certain features characteristic of Provençal poetry—frustration and suffering, longing for death, exaltation of chastity, and avoidance of any sexual consummation of love—are symbolic, and explicable only in terms of Catharism.

This thesis is supported by an elaborate historical theory.

[1] *Passion and Society*, pp. 76–7.

From a conjectured 'fusion of Iranian Manicheism, Neo-platonism, and Mohamedanism in the vicinity of Asia Minor' in the ninth century,[1] it is suggested that there developed a courtly 'religion of love' in which erotic imagery was used to represent the union of the soul with the divine love—an idea so intolerable to Mohamedan orthodoxy that persecution followed. This courtly love, with its distinctive poetry, then moved westward, and eventually made its way through Spain into southern France. Finally it is supposed that the secret doctrines of Catharism, derived from this Eastern source, became connected with the Celtic legend of Tristan and Iseult, which was adapted so as to give veiled expression to the Manicheism of the Provençal heresy. Thus an erotic passion element gradually infiltrated into the mainstream of European culture.

This theory is vitiated by lack of historical foundation. De Rougement himself admits that

> . . . up to the present day there has been no means of ascertaining how Arab mysticism, together with its courtly rhetoric, was transmitted in less than a century to the initiates of the Church of Love, and from these to the poets of Southern France.[2]

Nor can favourable social conditions satisfactorily explain why the new love appeared in Provençe at the end of the eleventh century rather than in Asia Minor during the ninth. Further, there is no conclusive proof that the vocabulary of romantic love was due to a borrowing and literal interpretation of the erotic symbolism of the Catharist heresy; it could as well have been suggested by the Song of Songs, Ovid, or the erotic poets of Greece. But it is inconceivable that men should not have known how to express what was in their hearts; the literature of the new movement of the Spirit can hardly have owed much to existing models, and in any case, similarity between the

[1] *Passion and Society*, p. 115.   [2] *ibid.*, p. 120.

Provençal poems and Manichean erotico-mystical writings
need mean little, for all erotic imagery is more or less conventional and by no means extensive.

The fact that the historical evidence for this thesis is uncon-
vincing, however, ought not to detract from the importance
of some of the author's conclusions. Whatever its origin and
however it finds expression, there can be no doubt of man's
tendency to seek, through 'passionate' experience, the attainment of an infinite, ecstatic bliss. The disillusionment which
must attend his search for this experience only provokes him
to a more eager pursuit. Passion is antagonistic to marriage
and to all principles of honour and morality—and above all,
to the ideal of 'one flesh'. It exalts adultery and is entirely
erotic; it does not recognize *philia* or *agape*. De Rougement has
detected and analysed a dangerous passion-element in our
society, the effects of which show what great and subtle perils
attend any abandonment of a full and balanced conception of
love. To over-emphasize *eros* may not only destroy satisfactory
sexual relation, but may open a door to admit the most
pernicious of all heresies.

> The god Eros is the slave of death, because he wishes to
> elevate life above our finite and limited creature state. Hence
> the same impulse that leads us to *adore* life thrusts us into its
> negation. . . . Agape is aware that our terrestrial and tem-
> poral life is unworthy of adoration, and even of being
> killed, but that it can be accepted in obedience to the
> Eternal. For after all, it is here below that our fate is being
> decided. . . . In the next world we shall meet, not divinizing
> Night, but our Creator and Judge.[1]

De Rougement interprets the obstacles and difficulties which
comprise one of the universal ingredients of the love story
as symbolic expressions of this secret, passionate desire for
suffering and death. But against this it must be said that

[1] *Passion and Society*, p. 231.

obstacles and difficulties are not peculiar to the love story; they are common to all fiction, and it cannot seriously be maintained that they originate in a wish for death, or, in most cases, are even symbolic. Moreover, the obstacles and difficulties characteristic of the love story need no occult interpretation; they are generally conventional devices introduced in order to be overcome in a manner appropriate to the matter in hand. It is certain that the obstacles in the Greek romances cannot be explained as symbolic of any desire for death and the dark night of union with divine love, nor can those in the *Decameron* stories, *Persuasion*, or *Jude the Obscure*.

Although the interposition of obstacles is a convenient literary device inseparable from the good love story, it is not wholly artificial, however, since it ensures that fiction shall reflect human experience. The features which de Rougement interprets in conformity with his passion-theory can better be understood in relation to the tragic element in love-experience. Literature is always an image of life, and if, in the Romances, difficulties and delays to the consummation of love occur and the problems of sexual relation assume what appears to be a disproportionate prominence, the explanation can best be sought in the tragic nature of amatory experience, particularly after the eleventh century. Tragic situations were bound to arise when the new idea of love came into conflict with social, and specially matrimonial conventions which took no account of the emergence of a new personal relation and the mysterious, secret nature of sexual encounter. The Tristan legend is at least as much a social document as a veiled expression of passion and longing for death. There is nothing new in the Mark-Tristan-Iseult pattern; the novelty lies in the context in which Mark and Tristan stand in opposition, the one demanding recognition of, and the other defying established social usages. Not only the Tristan legend, but all love stories in which frustrations occur, reflect the tension inseparable from love which, in everyday experience, leads to tragic situations.

APPENDIX II

THE NEW TESTAMENT DOCTRINE OF SUBORDINATION

NOTHING in St. Paul's teaching has been more misunderstood than his idea of subordination in marriage:

> Wives, be in subjection unto your own husbands, as unto the Lord. For the husband is the head of the wife, as Christ also is the head of the church, being himself the saviour of the body. But as the church is subject to Christ, so let the wives also be to their husbands in everything.[1]

These words, misunderstood and judged from the standpoint of modern feminism or sentimentality, are repugnant to many, but they embody nevertheless an important and fundamental truth. A distinction must always be made between those passages where the Apostle expresses his own or a contemporary opinion, or is under the influence of ideas such as the imminence of the *parousia*, and those where he is concerned with principles. It is generally assumed that when he enjoins wives to be 'in subjection' to their husbands he writes as a man of his time, taking for granted the androcentricity of the contemporary social order, whereas in fact he is drawing attention to an invariable factor in sexual relation. He is concerned, not with woman's legal or social status, but with the operation within the 'one flesh' union of a principle of subordination which finds expression wherever human community exists, although its range is indeed almost universal.[2] What St. Paul says of the wife's place in marriage can only be said because of

[1] Eph. 5.22–4.
[2] It is, of course, possible that a low standard of marriage in Asia Minor or some abuse by wives of their new Christian liberty may have impelled St. Paul to consider subordination in marriage, as W. Lock suggests, *The Epistle to the Ephesians* (Westminster Commentaries), p. 61.

her place as woman in the order of creation; only when her 'subjection' is isolated and not related to the general pattern of human subordination does it rightly become repugnant and intolerable.[1]

In the order of creation two kinds of subordination are exemplified. One is shown in the relation between the human and the sub-human orders, and is expressed in terms of superiority and inferiority; thus God has given man power over all things, having set them in subjection under his feet and invested him with governmental authority.[2] The other does not involve any inferior-superior relation, being a subordination *inter pares*, the subjection of equals one to another. Both are found in human communities, where the principle of subordination operates in a multitude of ways to differentiate between ruler and ruled, employer and employed, and so forth.[3] Without it, social stability is precarious, and equalitarian or communistic groups abolish it in a traditional form only to renew it in a fresh guise. Authority and obedience are essential in every community, and subordination of some kind is the only alternative to anarchy. But although it necessarily imposes upon men relative positions of superiority and inferiority, it can neither affect their essential equality nor enhance or diminish the intrinsic worth and dignity of the individual. Only when man's relations with man have been disorganized by sin does 'inferior-to-superior' subordination become prominent and often indistinguishable from tyranny or exploitation on the one hand, and subservience or oppression on the other.

Within the Church, too, both kinds of subordination exist. The faithful are enjoined,

[1] On St. Paul's use of *hupotassein* (=in Middle or Passive, 'to submit oneself' or 'to be subject'), see Armitage Robinson, *St. Paul's Epistle to the Ephesians*, p. 123.
[2] Cf. Ps. 8.4–8 and Ecclus. 17.2, etc.
[3] Cf. Rom. 13.1; also I Pet. 2.13 and Tit. 3.1. An important study of the effect upon Christian thought of the idea of subordination which figures prominently in the sociological thought of antiquity will be found in E. G. Selwyn, *The First Epistle of St. Peter*, pp. 101ff., and Essay II.

. . . obey them that have the rule over you, and submit to them: for they watch in behalf of your souls.[1]

Yet at the same time the entire common life and activity of Christians—their bearing towards those who stand outside the Church; their moderation in the things of the flesh; their rejoicing, in the power of the Spirit; their thanksgiving— proceed from a principle of spiritual order:

. . . submitting yourselves one to another in the fear of Christ.[2]

It is significant (though the fact is often overlooked) that St. Paul's words concerning this mutual subjection of the faithful immediately precede his teaching on marriage. As 'one flesh' Christians are evidently involved in a double subordination; the wife is to be 'in subjection'[3] to her husband and to 'fear' him, yet both must above all be subject 'one to another in the fear of Christ'.

In marriage as a natural ordinance we find an unilateral subordination; male and female have been so constituted with reference to one another that their relative status can only be expressed in terms of the 'headship' of man and the 'subjection' of woman. This does not, of course, mean (as so many think) that woman is inferior to man and somehow lower in the scale of being, though it does imply that she is radically different from him. This distinction is intrinsic to the human race, and has not been imposed upon society or insinuated into sociological thought by a dominant masculine caste. It has nothing to do with the relative physical capacities of the sexes, and implies neither a depreciation of woman's achievements and

[1] Heb. 13.17; the verb here is *hupeikein*, which appears nowhere else in the N.T. or LXX. Its meaning in this connexion is the same as that of *hupotassein*.

[2] Eph. 5.15–21; cf. I Pet. 5.5*b*.

[3] The verb in verse 22 must be supplied from the *hupotassomenoi* of the preceding verse; some MSS., etc., have *hupotassesthōsan* or *hupotassesthe*. Verse 22 is thus dependent upon verse 21 both grammatically and for its sense.

her contributions to culture and learning, nor a refusal of her just claim to a full share in affairs and equality of opportunity with man. But education and emancipation can never alter the fact that she is, and remains woman, though they may well help her better to understand what it means to be woman. She has an unique vocation to fulfil and a special place in society to occupy, and to that end has been endowed by her Creator with distinctive capacities and character. Man's 'superiority', like her 'subjection', is also rooted in the will of God, and is attested by his possessing by nature faculties for organization, direction, and government which normally surpass hers. Woman's gifts are exercised in other but equally significant ways. So elementary a differentiation in function must necessarily undergo great modification with the advance of civilization and the increasing complexity of social life, but the principle remains unchanged. When man and woman are brought into relation, particularly in marriage, it is inevitable that he should find himself 'the head of the woman', and that she should find herself 'in subjection' to him. In other words, men and women and marriage are as God made and ordained them, and not otherwise.

But in considering 'inferior-to-superior' subordination the distinction between true and false relation must not be forgotten. Subordination may be according to the will of God, but it may also reflect the egocentricity of sinful man. It is therefore important to understand what the superordination of the 'superior' means. Man's dominion over the lower creation must be compensated by a responsible exercise of that dominion to the glory of God. In the Church, submission to spiritual authority must find its proper complement in the pastoral vigilance of those to whom the oversight of the flock of Christ has been committed. And so in marriage, the husband's rule and the wife's subjection must both be in love. As Christians they have already submitted to one another 'in the fear of Christ', in whom sexual distinction possesses no ultimate

meaning;[1] as husband, however, the man is the 'head' of his wife, and as wife, the woman is 'in subjection' to her husband. This relation of superordination and subordination is a type of the relation between Christ and the Church, in terms of which subjection takes on a new character; the wife must be to her husband as the spiritual Bride is to the heavenly Bridegroom, and the husband, as 'head', must love his wife like Christ who 'loved the church and gave Himself up for it'. Moreover, subordination is to be understood with reference to union in 'one flesh':

He that loveth his own wife loveth himself; for no man ever hated his own flesh; but nourisheth and cherisheth it, even as Christ also the church; because we are members of his body.[2]

St. Paul's teaching on marriage in the Epistle to the Colossians,[3] and his ecclesiastical regulations concerning the conduct of women, have contributed to misunderstanding of his idea of subordination. It should be remembered that in writing to the Colossians he is not concerned to set forth an ideal of Christian marriage and family life. He is addressing Gentile converts who appear to have had other failings than a predilection for an obscure gnostic heresy, and so refers briefly to certain faults prevalent among pagans. These, he insists, are not appropriate to Christians and must be renounced; there must be no bitterness, disobedience, and provocation, and the subjection of the wife must now be 'as is fitting in the Lord'—it must be a true Christian subordination (implying a true Christian superordination), and not the subservience commonly demanded of women in ancient times. In the Christian household there is no room for tyranny or servility, yet the wife must know and willingly take her proper place. It is anachronistic to expect St. Paul to speak of the

[1] Gal. 3.28.   [2] Eph. 5.28*b*–9.   [3] Col. 3.18–19.

'happiness of mutual love',[1] but his words imply a much higher level of relation than many have been prepared to allow.[2]

In forbidding women to pray or to prophesy unveiled[3] St. Paul again invokes the principle of subordination. It does not matter whether this prohibition was justified, or whether it related only to certain churches[4] and to first-century discipline;[5] it is interesting simply because the Apostle does not appeal to custom in connexion with veiling, but sees even this small question in the light of the constitution of the order of creation. Man is 'the image and glory of God', and in the scale of order stands above woman, who is 'the glory of the man', being of him and created for him.[6]

There are two passages which contradict what St. Paul says here, and which may be spurious. In the same Epistle women are enjoined to 'keep silence in all the churches',[7] and in I Timothy they are forbidden to teach.[8] The former prohibition is enforced by an appeal to the 'law',[9] but the latter is related to the principle of subordination. A woman teaching involves the contradiction that she is thus given 'dominion over a man', and this cannot be permitted. In I Peter also wives are told to be 'in subjection' to their husbands, and their 'chaste behaviour' must be 'coupled with fear'.[10] These passages, and especially the last, show closer affinities with contemporary ideas of the status of woman than with the idea of subordination in Eph. 5 and I Corinthians 11, though even in Ephesians

[1] See the criticism of this passage by J. Weiss, *The History of Primitive Christianity*, p. 582.

[2] In both Eph. 5.25 and Col. 3.19 the phrase is *agapate tas gunaikas*. *Agapan*, or the Christian, is a word of deep and rich content.

[3] I Cor. 11.3–16.

[4] I Cor. 11.16 suggests that it was not so restricted.

[5] St. Paul's injunction was based upon customs and canons of propriety which have long been obsolete and meaningless. It clearly relates only to women at worship (I Cor. 11.5), and not to their presence in church on other occasions. No one would seriously claim that it should be enforced to-day.

[6] Cf. Gen. 2.21–3 and 18.　　　[7] I Cor. 14.34–5.　　　[8] I Tim. 2.12f.

[9] Presumably Gen. 3.16: 'Thy husband . . . shall rule over thee'; cf. in this connexion Kierkegaard on the 'quietness' of women and the power of silence, *For Self-examination*, pp. 70–1.

[10] I Pet. 3.1–2 and 5–7; see E. G. Selwyn, *op. cit., ad loc.*

there are signs of perplexity and hesitancy in the face of all the implications of the Christian view of woman and marriage.[1]

The Genesis creation and Fall narratives account for the difference between true and false subordination. Woman was 'taken out of man' to be his help, and her subjection to him in the fellowship of the 'one flesh' was a true subjection. But their relation was so altered by sin that the wife had to submit to the rule of her husband[2]—a rule which often meant a subjection to his domestic tyranny which her 'desire' towards him alone rendered tolerable.[3] So, through the obscuring of the real nature of the 'one flesh' union by sin, there gradually developed the marriage situation which, by historical times, had become almost universal. As a result of the restoration of his nature in Christ, however, man is able to realize the original ideal of marriage, and to understand subordination in terms of the mystical union between Christ and the Church.

In I Corinthians St. Paul seems to see the principle of subordination extending even into the eternal order:

. . . all things are yours; . . . and ye are Christ's; and Christ is God's.[4]

. . . the head of Christ is God.[5]

. . . when all things have been subjected unto him, then shall the Son also himself be subjected unto him, that God may be all in all.[6]

His language, however, is that of pre-Trinitarian thought, and it is not easy to determine precisely what relation he believed to subsist between Father and Son in Their eternal being. He appears to anticipate the theory of the Cappadocian Fathers, who attributed to the First Person of the Trinity a sort of

---

[1] A. Oepke (article on *gunē* in Kittel's *Theol. Wörterbuch*, i, p. 785) notes in St. Paul 'a strong tension between a "progressive" and a "Jewish-reactionary" attitude'.

[2] Gen. 3.16.   [3] *ibid.*   [4] I Cor. 3.21-3.   [5] I Cor. 11.3.   [6] I Cor. 15.28.

logical priority as the *principium* or 'Fount of Godhead' who in the eternal act of generation communicates His divinity to the Second Person. This subordinationism has been attacked by Dr. Leonard Hodgson,[1] but the plain language of the New Testament certainly seems to suggest it, and St. Paul appears to have understood the Son's relation to the Father as one involving both equality and subordination. Discussion of this problem, however, does not fall within the scope of this study.

To conclude: Scripture represents the creation as hierarchical in structure, and St. Paul sees the relation between man and woman as one determined by this principle of order. When brought together as 'one flesh' that relation still persists, and can only be expressed in terms of 'headship' and 'subjection'. It is radically conditioned, however, by the incorporation of husband and wife into Christ and by the interpretation of their union as significant of the union between the Church and its Head. St. Paul went no further; indeed, it would have been difficult for him to do so. But while affirming the principle of subordination and superordination as he understood it, it needs to be remembered that even in non-Christian marriage the *henosis* of man and woman introduces another and in some respects conflicting relational principle, and that always hierarchical order, personal equality and personal freedom must be held in tension. The true union of husband and wife in 'one flesh' does not abolish subordination and superordination between them, but provides that context of love in which both order and freedom can find their fulfilment in personal relation.

[1] In his Croall Lectures, *The Doctrine of the Trinity*; see esp. pp. 100–3 and 171–3.

SELECT BIBLIOGRAPHY

ABRAHAMS, I.: *Studies in Pharisaism and the Gospels* (First Series), Cambridge, 1917.

ANDREWES, LANCELOT: *The Works of . . .* , (Library of Anglo-Catholic Theology), 11 vols. Oxford, 1841-1854.

BECON, THOMAS: *The Booke of Matrimony*, London, 1564.

BERDYAEV, NICHOLAS, [Trans. Natalie Duddington]: *The Destiny of Man*, London, 1937.

BRIGHTMAN, F. E.: *The English Rite*, 2 vols. London, 1915.

BRUNNER, EMIL [Trans. Olive Wyon]: *The Divine Imperative*, London, 1942.

BUBER, MARTIN [Trans. R. Gregor Smith]: *I and Thou*, Edinburgh, 1942.

BURNABY, JOHN: *Amor Dei*, London, 1938.

CHAVASSE, CLAUDE: *The Bride of Christ*, London, 1939.

COMBER, THOMAS: *Works*, 7 vols. Oxford, 1841.

COSIN, JOHN: *The Works of . . .* , (Library of Anglo-Catholic Theology), 5 vols. Oxford, 1843-1855.

CREIGHTON, LOUISE: *The Life and Letters of Mandell Creighton*, 2 vols. London, 1904.

DOMS, HERBERT [Trans. G. Sayer]: *The Meaning of Marriage*, London, 1939.

DONNE, JOHN: *The Works of . . .* , 6 vols. London, 1839.

FOWLER, W. WARDE: *Social Life at Rome in the Age of Cicero*, London, 1908.

GILSON, E. [Trans. A. H. C. Downes]: *The Mystical Theology of St. Bernard*, London, 1940.

GORE, CHARLES: *The Sermon on the Mount*, London, 1905.

HADDAN, A. W., and STUBBS, W.: *Councils and Ecclesiastical Documents . . .* , 3 vols. Oxford, 1869-1878.

HALL, JOSEPH: *The Works of . . .* , 12 vols. Oxford, 1837-1839.

HAMMOND, HENRY: *A Practical Catechism* (Library of Anglo-Catholic Theology), Oxford, 1847.

HEFELE, C. J. [Trans. W. R. Clark]: *A History of the Christian Councils*, 5 vols. Edinburgh, 1883-1896.

HODGSON, LEONARD: *The Doctrine of the Trinity*, London, 1944.

HOOPER, JOHN: *Early Writings of . . .* , (Parker Society), Cambridge, 1843.

—— *Later Writings of . . .* , (Parker Society), Cambridge, 1852.

HOPF, CONSTANTIN: *Martin Bucer and the English Reformation*, Oxford, 1946.

HOW, F. D.: *Bishop Walsham How*, London, 1898.

JENKINS, DANIEL T.: (ed.) *The Doctor's Profession*, London, 1949.

JEWEL, JOHN: *The Works of . . .* , (Parker Society), 4 vols. Cambridge, 1845-1850.

KIERKEGAARD, SØREN A. [Trans. W. Lowrie]: *For Self-examination*, Oxford, 1941.

KINGSLEY, F. E.: *The Letters and Memories of Charles Kingsley*, 2 vols. London, 1894.

KIRK, KENNETH E.: *Marriage and Divorce*, London, 1948 (2nd. ed.).

LACEY, T. A.: *Marriage in Church and State*, London, 1912. [Revised R. C. Mortimer, London, 1947.]

LATHBURY, D. C.: (ed.) *Correspondence on Church and Religion of William Ewart Gladstone*, 2 vols. London, 1910.

LEWIS, C. S.: *The Allegory of Love*, Oxford, 1938.

LLOYD, C.: (ed.) *Formularies of Faith . . .* , Oxford, 1825.

LOCK, W.: *The Epistle to the Ephesians*, London, 1928.

MACMILLAN, A. T.: *What is Christian Marriage?*, London, 1944.

MERSCH, E. [Trans. A.B.]: *Love, Marriage, and Chastity*, London, 1939.

MESSENGER, E. C.: *Two in One Flesh*, 3 vols. London, 1948.

MOORE, G. F.: *Judaism*, 2 vols. Harvard, 1932.

MORTIMER, R. C.: See Lacey, T. A.

NASH, A. S.: (ed.) *Education for Christian Marriage*, London, 1939.

NYGREN, A. [Trans. Hebert, A. G., and Watson, P. S.]: *Agape and Eros*, 3 vols. London, 1932-1939.

OEPKE, A.: Article on *gunè* in Kittel's *Theologisches Wörterbuch zum Neuen Testament*.

OLIVER, J. R.: *Psychiatry and Mental Health*, New York, 1936.

PIPER, OTTO: *The Christian Interpretation of Sex*, London, 1942.

REFORMATIO LEGUM ECCLESIASTICARUM, ed. Edward Cardwell, Oxford, 1850.

ROBINSON, J. ARMITAGE: *St. Paul's Epistle to the Ephesians*, London, 1903.

DE ROUGEMENT, DENIS [Trans. M. Belgion]: *Passion and Society*, London, 1940.

SANDFORD, E. G.: (ed.) *Memoirs of Archbishop Frederick Temple*, 2 vols. London, 1906.

SANDYS, EDWIN: *Sermons* (Parker Society), Cambridge, 1841.

SELWYN, E. G.: *The First Epistle of St. Peter*, London, 1946.

STAUFFER, E.: Article on *heis* in Kittel's *Theologisches Wörterbuch* . . .

SWETE, H. B.: *Theodore of Mopsuestia on the Minor Epistles of St. Paul*, Cambridge, 1880.

TAYLOR, H. O.: *The Mediaeval Mind*, London, 1919.

TAYLOR, JEREMY: *The Whole Works of* . . . , 19 vols. London 1847-1854.

THOMPSON, FRANCIS: *The Works of* . . . , 3 vols. London, 1913.

THORNDIKE, HERBERT: *The Theological Works of* . . . , 6 vols. (Library of Anglo-Catholic Theology), Oxford, 1844-1856.

THORNTON, L. S.: *The Common Life in the Body of Christ*, London, 1943.

TULLOCH, JOHN: *Rational Theology* . . . *in England in the Seventeenth Century*, 2 vols. London, 1874.

TYNDALE, WILLIAM: *Works* (Parker Society), 3 vols. Cambridge, 1848-1850.

WATKINS, O. D.: *Holy Matrimony*, London, 1895.

WEISS, J.: *The History of Primitive Christianity*, London, 1937.

WILKINS, H. J. *The History of Divorce and Re-Marriage*, London, 1910.

WILLIAMS, CHARLES: *He came down from Heaven*, London, 1938.

—— *The Figure of Beatrice*, London, 1943.

—— *Religion and Love in Dante*, London, n.d.

WILLIAMS, N. P.: *The Ideas of the Fall and of Original Sin*, London, 1927.

INDEX

ABELARD, PETER, 5, 10
ABRAHAMS, I., 86, 88 n. 1, 89
   n. 1 and 2, 90 n. 1
Adultery, 70-7, 81, 88-93, 99
   in Jewish law, 88-92
Agape, 3, 24-30, 127
AKIBA, R., 91 n.1
ALBERTUS MAGNUS, 56
AMBROSE, 54, 64 n. 2, 122
ANDREWES, LANCELOT,
   73
Androgyniety, 18
Anglican Divines, 6, 58, 64-5,
   73-7, 101-4, 122
Anglicanism, 8, 73, 95
Apostolic Canons, 120 n. 3
Apostolic Constitutions, 70 n.2,
   120 n. 3, 121
AQUINAS, ST. THOMAS, 57,
   64, 71, 72, 97
Asceticism, 56, 63
ATHENAEUS, 24 n. 2
ATHENAGORAS, 99 n. 1, 122
AUGUSTINE, 47, 48 n. 6, 52,
   54, 64 n. 2, 69, 70 n. 2, 99,
   100, 106, 110, 111, 114, 116,
   120 n. 5, 122

Basar, 44 n. 1
BASIL, 70, 120 n. 3, 122
BEATRICE, 14
BECON, THOMAS, 6. 7, 58,
   102
BERDYAEV, N., 3, 9, 10, 30,
   31 n. 1, 32 n. 1; 2; 3
Bona Matrimonii, 56, 57, 99, 100,
   101
Book of Common Prayer, 73,
   75, 101, 102, 103, 104, 105
BRIGHTMAN, F. E., 101 n. 2

BROWNING, ROBERT and
   ELIZABETH, 10
BRUNNER, E., 9, 10, 20 n. 1,
   21
BUBER, MARTIN, 10, 11,
   17 n. 1, 24 n. 1
BUCER, MARTIN, 74, 102
BURNABY, JOHN, 26 n. 1,
   27 n. 1

CALISTUS, 120
Canon Law, 45, 72, 73
Caritas, 19
CASSIAN, 114
Catharism, 125-126
'Causes' for which matrimony
   was ordained, 101-108
CHAVASSE, CLAUDE, 115
   n. 1
CHRYSOSTOM, JOHN, 120
   n. 3, 121
Civil ceremony of marriage, 68
CLEMENT of Alexandria, 120
   n. 3
Cohabitation, responsible and
   irresponsible, 69
COMBER, THOMAS, 73-4,
   85 n. 1
Communication in love, 22-3, 60
Confusio prolis, 73
Consent, 45-9, 52, 53
*Constitutions and Canons Eccle-
   siastical*, 1604, 73
Contraception, x
Corinthians, 51-2
COSIN, JOHN, 75, 102
Councils :
   Agde, 120 n. 5
   Arles, 70 n. 2
   Elvira, 70 n. 2

Councils—*continued*
  Irish Synod II., 70 n.2
  Laodicea, 122 n. 6
  Neocaesarea, 122 n. 6
  Quinisext, 120 n. 4
  Toledo, 122 n. 6
  Valence, 120 n. 5
Creation of Man, 44
CREIGHTON, MANDELL, 76
CUDWORTH, RALPH, 112
CYRIL of Jerusalem, 121

DANTE, 14, 60 n. 1
Debitum, 66
Divorce, 43, 70-96
DOMS, HERBERT, 65, 110, 111
DONNE, JOHN, 103
Dualism, 56

Engagement, 38-9
Eros, 24-30, 50, 127
Erós ouranios, 25
Erós pandēmos, 25
EPIPHANIUS, 70 n. 2
Epipsychidion, 14 n. 1
Eucharist, 65, 69, 113

Falling in Love, 11, 13, 14, 16, 17, 19
Family, 117-120
Fatalism, 24
Fidelity, 21-2, 35, 79, 80, 96
Fornication, 50-3, 70, 99
FOWLER, W. WARDE, 3 n. 4
FRANCESCA, 59
Freedom and personal conflict, 30-1

GILSON, E., 5 n. 1; 2; 4; 5
GLADSTONE, W. E., 75 n. 2
Gnosticism, 59
GORE, CHARLES, 76

GRATIAN, 71
Greek Anthology, The, 3
GREGORY THE GREAT, 48 n. 2, 54, 63
GREGORY NAZIANZEN, 122

HALL, JOSEPH, 74
HAMMOND, HENRY, 73
HEFELE, C. J., 70 n. 2
HELOISE, 5, 10
HERMAS, 121
HILLEL, R., 86, 87, 89, 91
HIPPOLYTUS, 121 n. 1
HODGSON, L., 136
Homily, *Of the State of Matrimony*, 102
HOOPER, JOHN, 74 n. 4, 102
HOPF, C., 102 n. 5
HOW, Bp. WALSHAM, 76
HUGO of St. VICTOR, 56

Indissolubility of marriage, 70-96
Institution of a Christian Man, The, 73 n. 2, 101, 114

JENKINS, DANIEL T., x
JEROME, 54, 63
JESUS—Teaching on Marriage and divorce, 43, 85-94
JEWEL, JOHN, 64
Joseph and Mary, marriage of, 48
JOSEPHUS, 89

KIERKEGAARD, S. A., 134 n. 9
KINGSLEY, CHARLES, 103, 104, 123
KIRK, K. E., 77
'Know,' 'Knowledge,' in Scripture, 62, 124
LACEY, T. A., 70 n. 2, 72, 73 n. 1, 90 n. 2, 105, 106 n. 1